BERLITZ

CÔTE D'AZUR

- A ☑ in the text denotes a highly recommended sight
- A complete A–Z of practical information starts on p.115
- Extensive mapping throughout: on cover flaps and in text

Printed in Switzerland by Weber SA, Bienne.

17th edition (1995/1996)

Although we make every effort to ensure the accuracy of the information in this guide, changes do occur. If you have any new information, suggestions or corrections to contribute to the guide, we would like to hear from you. Please write to Berlitz Publishing at one of the above addresses.

Text:	Suzanne Patterson and Meg Jump
Editor:	Delphine Verroest
Photography:	Pete Bennett
Layout:	Suzanna Boyle
Cartography:	Visual Image
Thanks to:	Robert Blackwell and the Offices de Tourisme of Nice, Cannes, Fréjus and Monaco for their help in the preparation of this guide.

Cover photograph:	*The old town of Menton*, © The Telegraph Colour Library
Photograph on page 4:	*The rocky, pine-green peninsula of Cap Ferrat*

CONTENTS

The Region and its People

The Côte d'Azur, the Riviera, the South of France – call it what you will – this, for more than a hundred years, has been one of the world's most idealized travel destinations. Written about, discussed at length, painted and photographed, it probably has as much – perhaps more – glamour, prestige, charisma and wealth as any coastline anywhere.

Real estate values equal any in Europe, if not the world, and with good reason. These days parts of the Côte d'Azur may be over-developed, over-crowded and over-exposed, but it is not over-rated. The setting is as beautiful as ever, and it still has undeniable magic and inimitable appeal.

The Côte d'Azur conjures up pictures of azure skies and brilliant blue seas, the perfect backdrop for palacial villas and exotic gardens. In decades gone by, this coastal stretch had the reputation of being a millionaire's playground; a fabulous private holiday-land for the rich, royal and famous. Princes and professional gambling rakes, society hostesses and Hollywood film stars, authors and artists came here to see and be seen. It has become a legend in its own lifetime, and perpetuates the myth with characteristic allure.

Strictly speaking the Côte d'Azur is a very specific and limited area, extending roughly from Cannes to Menton. In real terms, however, it includes everything from Cassis in the west to the Italian frontier in the east, including much of the mountainous hinterland. This corner of France encompasses a truly entrancing panorama of ever-changing landscapes – sun-baked beaches, elegant resorts, historic towns and picturesque ports, of course; but you can also discover precipitous cliffs and craggy outcrops, secret bays and hidden inlets, wild unexplored mountains and arid hillsides, vineyards, cypresses and silvery olive groves, medieval villages perched on hillsides as well as **5** ancient churches. Its past is charged with daring and adventure; and today's traveller will find that even with the advent of long-haul flights and autoroutes, certain corners of the Côte d'Azur are still well away from the tourist circuit.

To really savour life down here, try sitting in a small-town square whilst relaxing to the music produced by gurgling fountains and watching the desultory social life which unfolds in the shade of outsized plane-trees.

There is twice as much sunshine here as in Paris, even if out of season the climate is not always perfect. Winter has its share of cool or cold days, and any time of year the mischievous mistral wind can come raging down the Rhône valley, freshening the vivid hues of Provence, but also exhausting

Langue d'Oc

An offshoot of Latin, Provençal began to take shape in the 4th century. By the 11th century, it was widely spoken in the south, carried from Nice to Bordeaux by the troubadours. These roving ambassadors went from château to château, singing the praises of idealized love. Both in style and theme, their poetry influenced the development of Western literature.

The language was known as *occitan*, because 'oc' rather than the northern 'oïl' (which became *oui*) was the word for 'yes'. After the 14th century, *langue d'oc* started to break down into regional dialects. Then, in 1539, Francis I decreed that French should be used in all administrative matters, and that was really the end.

Today you may hear, but certainly not understand, a bit of Niçois, Monégasque or some other vestige of Provençal. Some expressions, like *lou vieux mas* (the old farmhouse), have worked themselves into everyday life.

inhabitants and discouraging beach-goers with its incessant, irritating roar.

Given the bright colours and the quality of the light, it's no wonder that artists since Fragonard have gravitated to the south. Monet, Matisse, Cocteau and Picasso are just a few who celebrated the Côte d'Azur in unforgettable masterpieces.

Tourism is the area's largest industry, but it is not the only one. Others include perfume, ceramics, glass, boat-building, and ready-to-wear clothing. In addition, the agricultural sector produces magnificent fruit and vegetables, olives and, of

Don your cool shades, pick a prime spot, and watch the world go by in Saint-Tropez.

course, olive oil, and wine for both domestic consumption and export. Since the mid-60s and the creation of the business park at Sophia-Antipolis, just outside Nice, the area has also become a major centre for high-tech industries.

Unfortunately, because of its success and the density of its population, this isn't altogether the best place to find **7**

Local colour: orange trees in fruit; boules, on the other hand never go out of season.

deserted beaches. Marseilles ranks as France's second-largest city and Nice ranks at number seven. With the influx of tourists, the coastal population increases to twice its normal size during the summer. The hinterland, however, has much to offer, including more peaceful spots.

As for the local people, they have more in common with the easy-going, voluble Italians than with their cousins to the north. They speak with a rather drawn-out, lilting accent and there are several local dialects, or patois, which are difficult for outsiders to understand. In reality, they are much like the genial characters found in Marcel Pagnol's novels. All in all, the general mood is carefree and life tends to proceed at its own leisurely pace.

Do as the locals do: enjoy the good food and wine, the lively atmosphere, the beautiful scenery and glorious sunny weather which bless the Côte d'Azur. For nowhere else will you find the unique blend that make this the world's most glamorous resort area.

A Brief History

The attractions of the Côte d'Azur were discovered very early on. Artefacts found at Beaulieu, Nice and the Grimaldi Grottoes, indicate that people lived here in palaeolithic and neolithic times.

More definite history begins around 1000BC with the Ligurians, colonizers from the south-east who settled along the coast. Four centuries later, the ubiquitous ships of Greece arrived and the Ligurians were forced to the east. These energetic Greek traders, the Phocaeans, founded Marseilles, La Ciotat, Antibes and Nice.

Then in 125BC the Romans marched in, determined to establish a passageway to their Iberian colony. They established *Provincia Narbonensis* (Provence), and founded several important cities, among which Narbonne, the capital, in 118BC, Aix in 123BC and Fréjus in 49BC, built by Caesar as a rival to Marseilles.

The Greeks brought civilization and agriculture – the olive tree, the fig tree and grape vines – to the area; the Romans introduced their administrative systems, law and agricultural methods. Roman influence lasted for nearly six centuries; and during this period of relative peace, roads, towns and cities burgeoned all over southern France.

The Dark Ages

Christianity spread gradually throughout the Mediterranean during the first centuries AD. In the 4th century, it became the official religion of the Roman Empire, and in 450 the Church of Provence was formally organized along the lines of Roman administration.

As the Roman Empire declined, successive waves of Germanic tribes swept through the area from the 5th to 7th centuries, breaking down the established order and leaving behind a state of chaos. The Franks prevailed, but Provence was more or less autonomous until the rule of Charles Martel. In several campaigns between 736 and 739, he took **9**

*B*uilt by Julius Caesar to rival Greek Massilia (Marseilles), Fréjus boasts a glorious Roman heritage – here, the Aqueduct.

empire was divided up according to a treaty among Charlemagne's grandsons: Provence fell to the lot of Lothaire I, and when his son Charles assumed control in 855, it became the Kingdom of Provence.

From the 8th century on, the coast was often attacked by North African Muslims, also known as Moors or Saracens. In 884, they even built a mountain base at La Garde-Freinet from which they raided and pillaged neighbouring communities. Before they were driven out in the 10th century by Guillaume le Libérateur, Count of Arles, the Saracens had forced many local overlords and their followers to retreat into the hills – the origin of the perched village strongholds which dot the Midi today.

control of Avignon, Marseilles and Arles, firmly establishing his authority over the area.

Charles Martel's grandson, Charlemagne, was King of the Franks from 768 to 814. His reign was one of relative stability, but his heirs squabbled over the domain. In 843, the

The Counts of Provence

The situation improved markedly under Guillaume and his successors. With the Saracens gone, the counts of Provence emerged as strong, independent rulers under the titular authority of the Holy Roman

10

HISTORICAL LANDMARKS

350BC	Greeks establish a trading post at Nikaia (Nice).
49BC	Julius Caesar creates a new port at Fréjus.
1388	County of Nice becomes separate from France.
1521	Plague throughout the region.
1731	First English visitors to 'winter' in Nice.
1793	Nice returns to France but taken back by Savoy in 1814.
1814	Napoleon sails from Saint-Raphaël to exile in Elba.
1824	Nice's Promenade des Anglais built.
1834	Lord Brougham discovers Cannes.
1860	The County of Nice finally rejoins France.
1873	First Nice Carnival in two weeks prior to Lent.
1878	Casino opens in Monte Carlo.
1892	Artists' colony formed in Saint-Tropez.
1902	Hôtel Carlton opens in Cannes.
1912	Hôtel Negresco opens in Nice.
1920s	Saint-Tropez 'discovered' by writer Colette.
1942	Italy occupies Côte d'Azur on behalf of Germany.
1944	Southern France liberated by Allies.
1946	First major Cannes Film Festival.
1949	Matisse begins work on Rosary Chapel in Vence.
1956	Prince Rainier and Grace Kelly married.
1965	Creation of Nice University and Sophia-Antipolis.
1966	Work begins on marina complex in Port Grimaud.
1973	Picasso dies at his home in Mougins.
1986	Work starts on Arenas – the business centre of Nice.
1987	New high-speed train link between Paris and Nice.
1989	New marina complex in Port Fréjus opens.
1992	Extension of Nice Airport.

Empire. Trade and cultural activity revived, and the 12th and 13th centuries were the heyday of the troubadours, the period when Provençal became the most important literary language of western Europe.

In the 12th century, Provence passed to the counts of Toulouse and was then divided with the counts of Barcelona. One particularly able Catalonian ruler, Raimond Bérenger V, reorganized and unified the *Comté* of Provence into a ministate. The people of Provence received both commercial benefits and greater liberty from their ambitious new ruler who also became King of Naples and Sicily. In 1246, links with France were reinforced when

*F*réjus remembers its revolutionary son, Sieyès (above); Grimaud preserves its medieval past (right).

Raimond Bérenger's daughter, Beatrix, married Charles of Anjou (brother of the French King Louis IX).

In the 14th century, the house of Anjou gained control, while other powers claimed new territories. One such was the French-backed Pope Clément V who, shunning Rome, made Avignon his residence in 1309. The ensuing period was a golden age for the city, which became a great cultural centre. It remained the religious capital until 1377, when Pope Gregory XI returned to Rome. After his death, however, the 'Great Schism' arose between Italian and French factions, when two and sometimes three popes (one in Avignon) held court. The schism did not come to an end until 1417.

Provence Becomes French

After various changes of ruling powers, the larger part of Provence (including Aix and Marseilles) came back under the control of the dukes of Anjou. Under the rule of 'Good King René', last heir to the Anjou house, Provence's economy, arts and literature flourished. René left his domain to his nephew, who in turn named Louis XI, King of France, his successor. Thus Provence became part of France in 1481. Nice, however, went its separate way. It had formed an alliance with the dukes of Savoy in 1388, and remained Savoyard – with a few interruptions – until 1860.

The early 16th century was marked by strife between Francis I of France and Charles V, the Holy Roman Emperor. After an early victory in Milan (1515), the French monarch was driven out of Italy and imprisoned. Then it was the turn of Charles to invade Provence. In 1536, he took Aix and had himself crowned King of Arles before being forced into a disastrous retreat.

Acting as go-between in 1538, Pope Paul III managed to get both sides to sign the Treaty of Nice, a precarious armistice at best. Never deigning to meet, each party convened separately with the pope in Nice. The truce didn't last.

In 1543, helped by the Turkish fleet, Francis I bombarded Nice, allied to his rival through the house of Savoy. After a valiant struggle, Nice repelled the invaders, returning to the realm of the house of Savoy.

Wars and Revolutions

Meanwhile Europe had become the scene of fierce religious conflicts caused by the rise of Protestantism. The confrontations were especially bloody in the south of France. In 1545 more than 20 'heretic' villages (north of Aix) were levelled by order of Francis I; the years that followed saw much violence on both sides. Finally, King Henri IV's conversion to Catholicism and the Edict of Nantes (1598), grant-

*R*oyal pomp: cannon ready to fire on Antibes' Château Grimaldi and (right) the changing of the guard in Monaco.

ing religious freedom to the Protestants, palliated the situation. (It was revoked by Louis XIV in 1685.)

In the 17th century, Cardinal Richelieu, Louis XIII's all-powerful adviser, made the consolidation of the French state his priority. Measures to increase centralization and introduce new taxes gave rise to much agitation, and even outright rebellion in the case of Marseilles. Louis XIV brought the troublesome city to heel in 1660, by imposing additional contributions and restrictions. **15**

At the same time, Marseilles and Toulon were converted into major ports as protection against the Spaniards.

During the 17th and 18th centuries, Provence was the battleground for numerous disputes, both domestic and foreign. France took and lost Nice several times, but eventually gained some additional territory from the Duke of Savoy. However, stagnation set in as power centred more and more on Versailles and Paris. To add to the gloom, another outbreak of the plague swept through Provence in 1720, claiming 100,000 lives.

Like the rest of France, Provence had good reason to feel disgruntled by the end of the 18th century. Bad crops, poor administration and the distant court's constant drain on finance bred resentment. In July 1789, riots and massacres occured throughout the south.

In the administrative reorganization of France in 1790, Provence was divided into three *départements* – Var, Basses-Alpes, Bouches-du-Rhône – but the population was still starving, and fighting continued between royalists and republicans. Worse was to come in 1794 when royalist extremists initiated the 'White Terror' in Orange, Marseilles and Aix, slaughtering their Jacobin opponents. A state of lawlessness prevailed in some areas.

Napoleon in the South

Profiting from the disarray, the English easily took Toulon in 1793. Napoleon Bonaparte, an obscure captain at the time, distinguished himself in the recapture of the city. Promoted to general, he launched his Italian campaign from Nice (annexed by France from 1793 to 1814) in 1796.

Two years later, Toulon was the starting-point for his sensational Egyptian campaign, and when he returned in 1799, he landed triumphantly at Saint-Raphaël. You can see a small

Tourism is not the sole industry of the Côte d'Azur. The capital of perfume happens to be Grasse.

pyramid there erected to commemorate his victories.

However, his empire was unpopular in Provence: taxes and conscriptions were detested, and the blockade of Marseilles proved disastrous for trade.

Napoleon passed through Saint-Raphaël again in 1814 – but this time in disgrace, ignominiously escorted by Austrian and Russian troops on his way to exile on Elba. He es-caped from his island prison a year later, landing at Golfe-Juan and returning to Paris via Cannes, Grasse, Digne and Gap – a road now known as the Route Napoléon.

The restoration of the monarchy in 1830, in the shape of Louis-Philippe I, was greeted with something like relief. The revolution of 1848, however, took the south of France by storm, as peasants demanded

Follies of Fashion

The English were the first to make the Côte d'Azur fashionable in the late 18th century, finding the winter climate much to their taste. Nice – and particularly Cimiez – was their favourite haunt until Lord Brougham took a fancy to Cannes in 1834.

When at the end of the century, French painter Paul Signac discovered Saint-Tropez, other artists and writers joined him.

By the beginning of the 20th century, the Côte d'Azur was the playground of international 'high society' – princes, eastern potentates, heads of state, society hostesses, French courtesans, all made merry every night of the hectic winter season with gambling in the casinos, masked balls, gargantuan dinners and fantastic parties.

Escaping prohibition back home, the Americans arrived in the early 1920s, lured by the glamour of the coast and the low cost of an extravagant lifestyle. Based at Juan-les-Pins, they created the 'golden age' – introduced jazz and crazy dances, indulged in wild parties and set the vogue for summering in southern France.

the right to the land. The monarchy was deposed and replaced by the 2nd Republic.

By 1848, Napoleon III had come to power. In 1860 the house of Savoy gave up Nice in return for the Emperor's help in ousting the Austrians from the northern provinces of Italy. In a plebiscite, the Niçois overwhelmingly proclaimed their desire to join France, although Monaco stayed apart as a hereditary monarchy (see p.41). A year later, Monaco sold all rights to Menton and Roquebrune, which had also voted to join France.

The 20th Century

Southern France was scarcely involved in World War I, although there was conscription.

However, it could not escape World War II. In 1940, the Italians opened hostilities against France and succeeded in taking Menton. The Vichy Government of Marshal Pétain was left to govern the rest of the area until the Germans took over at the end of 1942, with the Italians occupying the Côte d'Azur. Before the Germans arrived, however, the French scuttled their own fleet at Toulon, blocking that all-important harbour.

As the American, British and Allied forces approached from North Africa and Italy, the Germans put up blockhouses and barbed wire on the beaches; Saint-Tropez was dotted with mines. Then on 15 August 1944, the long-awaited landings began, led by General Patch's 7th Army. The Americans swarmed over the beach to Saint-Raphaël and destroyed the blockhouses. The following day General de Lattre de Tassigny landed with his Free French troops at Saint-Tropez. Provence was free.

The post-war years were marked by the depopulation of inland Provence and the population boom of Marseilles, fuelled by the return of French settlers from Algeria in 1962. In the 1960s, too, the bikini made its first appearance on the coast, heralding a new mood of optimism. Business started to skyrocket. So did a building and tourism boom, which just hasn't stopped to this day.

The most glamorous hotels, the lushest palm trees – Nice's Promenade des Anglais has it all.

Where to Go

Nice

Pop. 338,000

Nice is like a rich dowager of simple origins who never lost her common touch. It's a vibrant, important city, boasting France's second largest airport, an opera house and excellent philharmonic orchestra, a university, several good museums, and shops, hotels and restaurants to rival the world's best.

Phocaeans from Marseilles settled here in the 4th century BC, and the name Nikaia (Nice) may have come from *nike*, the Greek word for victory. When the Romans marched in two centuries later, they headed for the healthier climes of Cimiez, where they founded a city.

Nice broke away from the rest of Provence in 1388, when it was annexed by the house of Savoy (see p.14). When Provence joined France in 1841, Nice stayed apart. (It joined France officially in 1860.) In the meantime, history ran its course: in the 15th century, the hill now known as **Le Château** supported a fortified castle, and beneath it a city grew up (now the **vieille ville**).

In 1631, Nice was almost wiped out by the plague – but survived. In 1796 Napoleon Bonaparte used the city as a base during his Italian campaign. Known as a winter resort in the late 1700s, Nice saw its touristic career take off in the next century with the arrival of the English and their queen, Victoria. Today, the city ranks as the unofficial capital of the Côte d'Azur.

It's easy to find your feet: old Nice clusters around Le Château, stretching as far as Boulevard Jean-Jaurès. Place Masséna marks the start of the modern city and its main thoroughfare, Avenue Jean Médecin. To the north is Cimiez and to the south, lining the seafront, is the Promenade des Anglais.

PROMENADE DES ANGLAIS

Any visit to Nice passes along this splendid palm-tree-lined 5km- (3-mile) long boulevard.

CÔTE D'AZUR HIGHLIGHTS

Cannes. The place to see and be seen. Stroll along La Croisette with its fashionable hotels and fine sandy beaches; window shop in chic boutiques; or sip a cool drink at a pavement café and indulge in some leisurely people-watching. Alternatively take a boat trip to the Iles de Lérins or cruise around the Corniche d'Or (the coast west of Cannes). (See p.54)

Cassis and Les Calanques. A unique 5,000ha (12,355 acres) site of wild semi-arid coastline characterized by craggy outcrops and fjord-like inlets (*calanques*) of white limestone. View the *calanques* by boat from picturesque Cassis. For hikers there is an 11-hour walk along the coast from Marseilles to Cassis. (See p.90)

The Estérel. This area offers spectacular wild scenery and culminates at Mont Vinaigre, at 616m (2,020ft). A tortuous coastal road offers great views of craggy red rock and semi-tropical vegetation. There are numerous paths for mountain bikes and hikers. (See p.61)

Fréjus. A lively market town, originally an episcopal city, with a splendid 13th-century fortified cathedral and magnificent galleried cloisters. There is also the Roman arena which dates from the 1st century AD. (See p.63)

Monaco. A fairytale setting for a city renowned for its casino and the personal wealth of its inhabitants. Visit the old town on Monaco Rock with the Prince's Palace; there is a daily changing of the guard. In Monte Carlo (the 19th-century area), admire the flamboyant neo-Baroque architecture and the Casino. (See p.38)

Old Nice. The old town is a warren of narrow streets with hundreds of fascinating shops and restaurants. There is also the added spectacle of the markets in Cour Saleya and Place Saint-François, with their explosions of colour and confusion. Chapelle de la Miséricorde houses many major 15th- and 16th-century altar paintings. You should also visit Palais Lascaris – a fine Baroque mansion – and the Cathedral of Sainte-Réparate, which contains the very beautiful Saint-Sacrement Chapel. For a spectacular view over Nice and the Baie des Anges, climb to the summit of Le Château. (See p.24)

*I*n Nice, ride around in style in the Jardin Albert-Ier, or. take a stroll around the old port (right).

It starts in the west outside the airport and the ultra-modern hotel and business complex of Arenas. Next door is the exotic flower-filled Parc-Phoenix containing the largest single-span glasshouse in the world, at some 7,000sq m (75,000sq ft).

For most of the way the Promenade – thus named because in the 1820s the widening of a coastal path was paid for by local English residents – runs beside the Mediterranean shoreline (with both public and private beaches) of the Baie des Anges. Half way along is the legendary **Negresco** – a stunning Belle Epoque hotel with an imposing rococo façade, colourful turrets and costumed doormen. The Negresco's Chantecler Restaurant is reputed to be one of the finest in Europe (see p.70).

At the end of the Promenade, where it joins the Quai des Etats-Unis, is a flowered park, the **Jardin Albert-Ier**, with an 18th-century Triton fountain and a modern outdoor theatre. Behind the gardens, running parallel to the Promenade des Anglais, is a shopping area, mostly reserved for pedestrians.

North-east of the park is the **Place Masséna**, a picturesque square of arcaded buildings in ruddy stucco, built in 1835.

LA VIEILLE VILLE

You can enter the old city from the seaside (Quai des Etats-Unis) or the Place Masséna.

From this latter direction, proceed past the **Opéra** and its elaborate 19th-century façade. Continue to the **Cours Saleya** (the name comes from 'salt', which was at one time sold in bulk here). This is where the flower market takes place, full of the colour and the scent of roses, tulips, dahlias and geraniums (from 6am to 4pm), and the fruit and vegetable market – just as picturesque, though more aromatic (from 6am to 1pm). Both markets are open daily except Monday when there is an antique and bric-à-brac market from 8am to 4pm.

On the quayside, the little pastel houses where fishermen used to live (mostly art galleries and restaurants now) are known as *ponchettes*, a provençal word meaning 'little rocks'. Opposite is the **Miséricorde** chapel. Built by the Black Penitents (a lay sect) in 1736, it contains an attractive

altarpiece by Mirailhet, *La Vierge de Miséricorde*.

Behind the Cours Saleya is the old world of Nice with its appetizing aromas, tiny shops spilling their wares onto the streets and excited voices talking Niçois, a form of Provençal that rolls like Italian. **Rue Droite** looks like a cramped alleyway now, but it used to be the main street in the Middle Ages. On the right is Saint-Jacques, the heavily decorated baroque church modelled after Il Gesù in Rome. Set back on the left is Sainte-Réparate cathedral (1650) with its handsome 18th-century belfry.

The **Palais Lascaris** (15, rue Droite) is a 17th-century town house that belonged to the Lascaris family until the French Revolution. Although small for a palace, the building has a handsome carved marble staircase and frescoed ceilings – don't miss the odd-angled carved door, built to swing shut automatically. On the ground floor is a beautifully preserved pharmacy, dating from 1738, complete with apothecary jars. The shop came from Besan-

çon, a gift of the Gould family (American industrialists).

Further on you'll find Place Saint-François with its nicely proportioned, late-baroque, former town hall. Every morning except Monday, a frenetic fish market takes over the square – gleaming with red mullet, sea bass and squid.

On Place Garibaldi, outside the old town, a stabile by Calder stands in front of the bus station. Opposite is the rather pompous **Musée d'Art Moderne**, grouping contemporary French and American artists of the avant-garde since the 1960s. Esplanade John-Fitzgerald-Kennedy, nearby, is the site of the **Acropolis**, Nice's impressive exhibition and conference centre.

LE CHÂTEAU AND THE HARBOUR

Though you won't find anything left of Nice's stronghold of the Middle Ages, destroyed in 1706, a visit to the 92m (300ft) summit of **Le Château** is pleasant nonetheless. Hardy walkers can climb the steps in

15 minutes, but a lift service also operates daily from 9am to 6pm from Quai des Etats-Unis. Alternatively, take the 'little white train' which runs from the Quai des Etats-Unis through the Cours Saleya and the narrow streets of the old town (see p.138). It is a highly enjoyable experience, especially if you leave the train at the top (it turns round and goes straight back down), have a drink in the café and come down by a later train. At the top there is a public park, with exotic pines and cacti – and a spectacular view of the colourful port on one side and the Baie des Anges on the other. The white stones you'll see are remnants of Romanesque religious buildings. Military buffs will be interested by the naval museum in the Tour Bellenda (closed Tuesday).

Filled with both pleasure and merchant boats, the **port** is always lively and lined with bars, cafés and restaurants specializing in the Niçois version of the famous Mediterranean fish stew – *bouillabaisse*.

From the north-east corner of the harbour, you can take the Boulevard Carnot to the extraordinary **Terra Amata** museum, located at number 25.

Carnival Cavortings

Nice's February Lenten carnival, or Mardi Gras, lasts for a festive two weeks. Begun as simple fêtes in the 13th century, the carnival was put on in splendid style in 1873.

Today crowds jam the boulevards, for the parades of floats in extravagant shapes and colours. The papier mâché used for the floats requires about a tonne of paper, plus 317kg (700lb) of flour. Masked parades and balls alternate with the battles of flowers and confetti. The climax is the Shrove Tuesday burning of King Carnival in effigy and a fireworks display, topped off by cannon volley from the castle hill.

25

Practically hidden under towering residential buildings, it contains a sizeable collection of prehistoric remains found in a sand dune when the land was being cleared for construction. Three hundred thousand years ago, men hunted on the shores which now lie under these recent buildings.

CIMIEZ

Originally built by the Romans, this hilly residential suburb was much favoured by the European aristocracy during the 19th century. Grandest of the many hotels and villas constructed at that time is the former Hôtel Excelsior Régina Palace – a favourite of Queen Victoria that was later converted into apartments. (The artist Matisse spent his later life in one of these.)

Within easy reach of Nice city centre (you can take bus no. 15 from Place Masséna), the route to Cimiez passes close to the **Musée Marc-Chagall** (see p.60) at the lower end of Boulevard de Cimiez. At the top of the boulevard is the **Régina Palace** and Villa des Arènes, the latter containing an archaeological museum and the **Musée Matisse**. Important works from all periods of Matisse's life are displayed with personal items from his studio (see p.60).

Behind the villa you can walk around the **Roman ruins**

*T*he Régina Palace owes its name to a most illustrious royal visitor: Queen Victoria.

Matisse and Chagall

Matisse (1869-1954) was born and brought up in the grey industrial north of France. He first visited Saint-Tropez in 1904 and was immediately seduced by the vibrant colours of the Côte d'Azur. His painting was transformed, characterized by the brilliance of his palette. From 1916 he spent part of every year working in Nice and in 1921 bought an apartment in the old town, later moving to Cimiez. From 1949-51 he worked on the Chapel of the Rosary at Vence – a gift to the Dominican nuns who cared for him during a long illness. The studio where he worked has been preserved and contains an important collection of paintings from all periods of his life (see p.60).

Marc Chagall (1889-1985) was born in Russia, studied art in St Petersburg and moved to Paris in 1910. Between the wars he worked on book illustrations of the Old Testament which reveal clear evidence of his interest in Russian folk painting. He became a French citizen in 1937 and from 1949 until his death, spent much time on the Côte d'Azur at Vence, where he decorated the cathedral baptistry in 1979. His work is on permanent display at the Maeght Foundation and a major collection of biblical paintings are exhibited at Cimiez (see p.60).

(2nd and 3rd centuries AD), including the remains of a small amphitheatre and part of the Roman bath complex. The Musée d'Archéologie is also situated here (see p.60).

On the eastern side is a **Franciscan monastery** with a late Gothic church (extensively restored in the 17th century) containing three remarkable altar pieces painted on wood in the 15th century – the work of Louis Bréa. The church is open 10am to noon and 3 to 5pm, closed over the weekend. Both Matisse and Dufy are buried in the adjoining cemetery.

NICE EXCURSIONS

Nice is an excellent starting point for short trips along the Côte d'Azur and into the wonderful hinterland.

If you enjoy spectacular scenery and mountain driving, take the day-long tour featuring the twin gorges of Daluis and Cians. Leaving Nice on the RN202, you will follow the River Var and pass through numerous medieval villages.

Entrevaux, a lovely fortified town with a drawbridge, ramparts and a hilltop citadel, is well worth a visit. Then head for Guillaumes via the grandiose **Gorges de Daluis**, outstanding for their depth and red schist colouring. Stops then include the ski resort of **Valberg** and the old Alpine town of **Beuil** before entering the **Gorges du Cians**, where the river plunges 1,600m (5,250ft) as it flows into the Var.

Another spectacular excursion goes to the Vésubie Valley with its green mountain slopes and rushing waters fed by melting snows. Visit **Saint-Martin-Vésubie**, located on a

The clean, pure lines of the Matisse Museum provide the perfect backdrop for the artist's colourful work.

spur between two torrential streams. Nearby, at the Mercantour National Park, don't miss the beautiful **Vallée des Merveilles** (open July to October) with its prehistoric rock engravings.

The sinuous road leading up to the Madone d'Utelle, at 1,174m (3,850ft) passes by an interesting 18th-century church in **Utelle**. At the summit you'll find a breathtaking view and a sanctuary founded in AD 850 (rebuilt in 1806).

The Corniches

The pre-Alpine mountains drop down to the sea between Nice and Menton, creating as they do some spectacular scenery.

The highest views are from the route known as the **Grande Corniche**, built by Napo-

leon along the ancient Aurelian Way. The **Moyenne** (middle) **Corniche** offers a vivid contrast between rocky cliffs and sea. The **Corniche Inférieure** (lower), or Corniche du Littoral, runs along beside the sea and can be very crowded in summer, but does include some very worthwhile places to visit.

CORNICHE INFÉRIEURE

Villefranche, 6km (4 miles) east of Nice, is one of the most sheltered Mediterranean harbours. Clinging to a steep slope under the road, Villefranche offers instant charm, with its yellow, pink and red stucco or brick houses packed against the hill, its plunging alleyways and staircases and the covered **Rue Obscure** that snakes down to the sea. The **29**

quayside cafés are well placed for watching pleasure boats and for a view of Cap Ferrat, pointing off to the left like a green finger.

On the right, below the town's old citadel (built for the Duke of Savoy in 1560), is the 14th-century Chapelle Saint-Pierre, also known as the **Cocteau chapel**, since writer-artist Jean Cocteau decorated it in 1956. The bold, pastel drawings completely fill the small vaulted chapel with scenes of fishermen, plus biblical episodes from the life of St Peter.

Further on lies the rocky, pine-green peninsula of **Cap Ferrat**. A short drive around will convince you that the rich really do appreciate privacy. The view is mostly of gates hinting of grandeur. The vast, cream-coloured villa that belonged to King Leopold II of the Belgians can only be seen from afar. Somerset Maugham lived in Villa Mauresque, also rather well hidden.

The best views are from the upper levels of the **Ephrussi de Rothschild Foundation** (or Musée Ile-de-France; open daily). Built between 1905-12 by Béatrice Ephrussi, née Rothschild, the pinkish Italian-style villa is the delirious assemblage of an insatiable art collector. While you'll admire a Coromandel screen and other beautiful *chinoiseries*, as well as examples of Renaissance, Louis XIII furniture and a few Impressionist paintings, the Foundation really shines in its French 18th-century pieces: the collection of Sèvres porcelain, composed of thousands of rare pieces and signed complete sets, is perhaps the largest in the world. The gardens surrounding the villa are no less extraordinary: the main one is French in style, but many others are inspired by countries further afield.

The house and gardens are closed on Sunday morning, all day Monday and throughout November.

Ochre, green and blue: the colours of the Mediterranean coastline find their perfect expression at Villefranche.

Not far away, the modest Cap Ferrat **zoo** is a favourite with children for its trained monkey shows – the *Ecole des chimpanzés*.

Saint-Jean-Cap-Ferrat is the port side of the peninsula, with a modern seaside promenade and an older fishing village; gifted artist Jean Cocteau decorated the marriage room of its small town hall.

Beaulieu – a favourite resort with the English during the last century – is today an elegant seaside town enjoying one of the mildest climates of the entire coast. There's a lively, bustling fruit and vegetable market every morning in the main square and ever-popular quayside bars and restaurants surround the resort's crowded, colourful marina.

Of particular interest is **Villa Kérylos**, which is one of the few great villas on the Côte d'Azur open to the public.

Built by scholar-musician-bibliophile Théodore Reinach in the early 20th century, it is acknowledged as the finest re-creation of an authentic Greek villa in the world. Designed to be an absolutely perfect replica, down to the most minute detail, the villa is constructed from marble, alabaster and ex-otic woods, and ancient Greek antiques (vases, statuettes, mosaics, etc) have been incorporated into the overall design.

Villa Kérylos is open to the general public every afternoon except on Monday and remains closed throughout November and the first week of December.

This fairytale residence – the Ephrussi de Rothschild Foundation – is the fitting repository for some of France's most delicate porcelain.

GRANDE CORNICHE

The **Grande Corniche** road goes all the way to Menton, via Roquebrune. You can stop off at **La Turbie**, or explore inland villages like Peille and Peillon (see p.37).

On a clear day, the **Belvédère d'Eze**, at 512m (1,680ft), offers a panoramic view of the coast, the Tête de Chien mountain over Monte Carlo, the old perched city of Eze below and, to the right, as far as Cap d'Antibes and the Estérel mountains.

La Turbie's star attraction is the **Trophée des Alpes**, a ruin with Doric columns standing guard over Monaco. Emperor Augustus built it in 6BC to celebrate victory over various battling peoples who had prevented the construction of a road between Rome and Gaul.

MOYENNE CORNICHE

One highlight of the **Moyenne Corniche** (the best road of the three) is the village of **Eze**, hanging at a gravity-defying angle above the sea, which is majestic and deep blue from this perspective. It rates as one of the most magnificent views on the coast. Medieval Eze is closed to traffic but not tourists, who flock here in all seasons, ambling around the tiny stone streets filled with souvenir shops. On the site of an old château, demolished in 1706 by Louis XIV, is a public garden full of exotic flowers and cacti.

Further on, the Moyenne Corniche skirts around Monaco (see p.38). Enjoy the stunning view at **Cabbé** before turning off for Roquebrune. Instead of **Roquebrune** ('brown rock'), the town should really have been called 'Roquerose' – for pink is the overriding colour here on a sunny day (caused by reflections from the sienna-red stucco buildings along the streets).

You can visit the dungeon of the fortified castle, built in the 10th century by the Count of Ventimiglia to fend off the Saracens. Stony and spartan, the ruin still looks very much the fortress, with walls ranging from 1.8 to 3.6m (6 to 12ft) in **33**

depth and a bedroom furnished with a blunderbuss.

Part of the Roquebrune municipality, the **Cap Martin** promontory is a millionaires' enclave, green with pine and olive trees, favoured in the last century when nobody cared much for sea-bathing (there is no beach).

Menton

Hot-point of the Côte d'Azur for climate, lukewarm for fun and games, Menton is especially appreciated by retired

The superb medieval village of Eze is also famed for its exotic garden (top).

people because of its warmth, simplicity and two casinos (the main one is a baroque gem).

Lemons flourish here, and it's no surprise that the locals like to tell their Adam-and-Eve legend: when they were chased from Paradise, Eve took along a lemon. After finding this new garden of Eden, she planted the 'immortal fruit', which sprang up all over the slopes under the greyish lime. In February there is a festival dedicated to the crop.

A long pebble beach and the Promenade George V lead to a 16th-century bastion, now the **Musée Jean-Cocteau**; further along is a jetty with a lighthouse and the modern Garavan harbour.

On Friday from 7.30am to 5pm there is an antiques market at the **Place aux Herbes**, with its arcades and three huge plane trees. From there you can go uphill to reach the heart of the Italianate **vieille ville**. Here the 17th-century **Eglise Saint-Michel** occupies a delightful square with a view right to Italy. Cocteau painted some bold and fanciful allegorical frescos in the marriage room of the town hall. The Musée Municipal contains odd bits of folklore, modern works and a few old bones.

Two public gardens in Menton are worth a look. The **Jardin Botanique**, arranged round a villa called Val Rahmeh, proves that everything can indeed grow in Menton – from a riot of roses to Mexican yucca, fuchsia and Japanese cane bamboo.

More curious is the **Jardin des Colombières**. Built by writer-painter Ferdinand Bac, the Hellenic-style villa (now converted into a modest hotel-restaurant) commands a splendid view. The terraced gardens out back are a romantic haven of flowered walks, punctuated by cypresses, ponds, fountains and statues.

MENTON EXCURSIONS

Around Menton, hikers can venture up through groves of gnarled olive trees, pine and scrub oak and finally the thick maquis scented with aromatic wild herbs.

A worthwhile inland excursion from Menton is 15 winding kilometres (9 miles) up into the mountains as far as **Sospel** – a small Alpine town of great charm on the banks of of the River Bévêra. This was the second most important town in the old County of Nice and although parts were badly bombed during World War II, the old medieval town remains intact with its arcaded streets and gaily painted houses.

Sights include the 13th-century church of Saint-Michel, an 11th-century bridge (restored in 1953) and – strangely enough – three perfectly preserved original carriages from the Orient Express (open daily; 20F). There is excellent walking in the area; full details are available from the tourist office, tel. 93.04.15.80. (You can also visit Sospel by train from Nice station. The journey takes just over an hour and the train continues first to the mountain town of Tende, then passes through a tunnel at the Col de Tende at 1,900m (6,232ft), before reaching Cuneo in Italy.)

For a full day out, you could continue north to **Col du Turini** – a pass at 1,600m (5,248ft) with some exceptional flora and stunning forested mountain scenery, plus a couple of hotel-restaurants. (Do take a sweater as it is chilly, even in midsummer). Then head south for a memorable drive via **Peïra-Cava** – a village (with skiing in winter) perched on a rocky outcrop between the valleys of the Bévêra and the Vésubie. Just outside the village look for a sign to **La Pierre Plate**, where there is a stone orientation table and wonderful views as far as the islands off the Cannes coast.

The road then passes the medieval village of **Lucéram**, **L'Escarène** (on the old salt route from Nice to Turin) and **Peillon** with its superb 15th-century frescos in the **Chapelle des Pénitants Blancs**. Return to the coast via the historic old town of **Peille** and the

M*enton, shrouded in the gentle torpor of the Midi, seems untouched by the passage of time.*

37

fortified village of **Sainte-Agnès**, which claims to be the highest of the local perched villages (guided tours every afternoon from June to September; and Saturday and Sunday afternoon October to May).

Look out, too, for **L'Annonciade**, a Capuchin monastery with a beautiful view; and the picturesque medieval towns of **Gorbio** and **Castellar**.

If you long for real Italian spaghetti, just cross the border to **Ventimiglia**. A visit here

should include the Romanesque cathedral, the baptistery (11th century) and the Friday street market, where stalls accept French francs as well as Italian currency. It is easier to travel by train than try to park in the town.

Monaco

Pop. 25,000

This fairytale princedom, an enclave rising from the rocks above the sea, is famed for its casino and wealth (residents pay no income tax). Monaco owes much of its current success to business-minded Prince Rainier and to the charm of the late Princess Grace.

The atmosphere here is both big city and miniature operatic. This is a crowded paradise, with a population density comparable to that of Hong Kong, and with cars jamming thor-

A jewel of a principality, Monaco is also a lively warren of cool, shady streets.

oughfares over the hills (use the public lifts which take passengers effortlessly up). The smartly uniformed Monegasque *gendarmes* have their work cut out keeping order.

You shouldn't get the idea that gambling is the only local attraction; a mere 5 percent of Monaco's revenue comes from the casino. Many other commercial and cultural activities take precedence. For one thing, Monaco is a music capital with a top European orchestra and ballet company, an opera house and a music festival. Then there's the motor rally and the **Grand Prix**, which set the sinuous streets roaring. Besides brilliant galas, Monaco holds a dog show, flower show and TV festival. It also boasts a successful soccer team and a radio station that beams all over Europe. Last but not least, philatelists have long admired the principality's beautiful stamps.

In brief: Monaco refers to the principality, geographically the historic peninsula-rock; Monte Carlo (Mt Charles) is the newer 19th-century area that curves out east of the rock.

In between lies La Condamine, a landfill flat area, comprising the harbour and modern business district. A fourth district, Fontvieille, is a new town built on reclaimed land to the west.

MONTE CARLO

All roads lead to the main **casino** (and opera), introduced by a neatly tended garden-promenade. Any resemblance to the Paris Opéra is more than coincidental, since architect Charles Garnier designed both.

A lavishly decorated foyer, full of frescos and voluptuous caryatids in 19th-century style, takes you in to the opera. Off to the left are the gambling rooms – if you can tear your eyes away from the roulette wheels, the ornate décor here is a sheer delight. Especially amusing is the Salon Rose, where painted, unclad nymphs float about the ceiling smoking cigarillos.

Next door stands the **Hôtel de Paris**, an equally opulent historical monument. Louis XIV's bronze horse in the entrance hall has so often been **39**

*M*onaco's opera could be mistaken for its Parisian sibling – architect Charles Garnier has a lot to answer for!

'stroked for luck' by gamblers that its extended fetlock shines like gold. The dining room has been brilliantly redecorated in Louis XV style and is the first restaurant in Monaco to be awarded three Michelin stars.

Across the square, you will find the lively Café de Paris, a popular rendez-vous that hums with the frantic whir of slot machines, helpfully installed for the use of gambling addicts between drinks.

Nearby, Monaco's **National Museum** is dedicated to a rather delightful doll museum. This whimsical spot houses a 2,000-piece collection from the 18th century to modern times. The villa-museum, designed by architect Charles Garnier, is a pink confection, perfect as a doll's house, nestled in a garden dotted here and there with statues by Rodin, Maillol and Bourdelle. Exhibits include tableaux and exquisitely outfitted dolls, while a series of automatons perform beautifully when the guard winds them up. There are extraordinary 'performances' by mechanical card-players, acrobats, dancers and a snake-charmer – slightly spooky but quite impressive. Children love it.

THE MONACO ROCK

A short ride up the hill from the centre of town, you'll find the **Palais du Prince** (bus or taxi recommended, as parking space is severely limited).

The Grimaldis still live here, but you can visit the palace from June to the middle of October. The tour includes a look at the magnificent 17th-century interior courtyard with its marble staircase and painted gallery, the **Galerie d'Hercule**.

There are several well-maintained rooms containing priceless antiques, paintings by Van Loo, Brueghel and Titian, a gallery of mirrors, royal family portraits and the elaborate bed where the Duke of York died in 1767.

The Grimaldis

The rock of Monaco was inhabited from the Stone Age onwards. In 1215, the Genoese built a fortress there, which the Guelf and Ghibelline factions disputed until finally, in 1297, the Guelfs, led by François Grimaldi, gained the upper hand. The Grimaldi family has hung on tenaciously ever since.

Treaties with powerful neighbours assured Monaco's independence over the years (except for a French interlude from 1793 to 1814). Roquebrune and Menton broke off from the principality in 1848 and were later bought by France. Looking for a new source of revenue, Monaco's ruler, Charles III, founded the Société des Bains de Mer in 1861 to operate gambling facilities. Charles then commissioned the construction of a casino and opera house. Hotels went up, and a railway line from the rest of the coast was soon extended to Monaco.

In spite of tricky legal tangles, Monaco has retained its independent (and tax-free) status, with open boundaries to France, free currency exchange (French money is almost always used) and a common post and telephone system with France.

Monaco is a pleasant place in which to live, but it's almost impossible to become a citizen – unless you can find some Monégasque ancestors.

Year-round, at 11.55am, you can watch the changing of the guard outside the palace. With fife and drums, much circumstance and little pomp, it's a good five minutes' worth of entertainment.

The **old town** is also located on the Monaco Rock. Along the narrow pedestrian streets riddled with souvenir shops, restaurants and other tourist attractions, a lively atmosphere prevails, ringing with the Italian inflections of Monégasque patois. On Rue Basse, you'll come across **L'Historial des Princes de Monaco** – a wax museum assembled in 1971 by a French Monacophile. From the earliest Grimaldi, François (see p.41), to the most recent – the three children of Princess Caroline – the beautifully costumed personages present a pleasant historical panorama. This quaint museum is open daily from 10am to 6pm; the entrance fee is 24F.

The **cathedral**, on Rue de l'Eglise, is a white, 19th-century neo-Romanesque monster, boasting a tryptich by Louis Bréa (right transept). Behind the high altar is the burial place of Princess Grace.

The **Musée Océanographique**, on Avenue Saint-Martin, is a formidable, grey-pillared construction, founded in 1910 by Prince Albert I, who spent the better part of his time at sea. It is now directed by Commandant Jacques-Yves Cousteau, the underwater explorer. In the basement aquarium, playful sealions, jaded turtles and thousands of small incandescent fish cavort. (The 60F entry charge makes it the most expensive museum to visit on the coast.)

The **Jardin Exotique** above the Condamine is worth visiting for its excellent view of the principality (take the lift from the port). Stepping stones lead you through a display of exotic plants – especially fierce-looking spiny cacti in thousands of varieties, from South America and Africa.

Close to the Jardin Exotique is the **Musée d'Anthropologie Préhistorique**, where you will see ancient bones from Menton and Monaco caves, plus ancient jewellery found in the Condamine. The 250 steps leading down to the *grottes* (or caves) will reward you with a cool promenade through lacy pinpoints of crystal-clear stalactites and stalagmites.

A little way off is the **Stade Louis-II**, one of Europe's biggest sports complexes, and the Princess Grace Rose Garden.

There's also a zoo – small, friendly but unspectacular, except for the good view.

If you just want to relax, however, go to Monte Carlo's **Larvotto Beach**, a top-quality man-made beach with imported sand, trees, shower facilities and a selection of bars and restaurants. It is also free.

At Monaco's Musée Océanographique, would-be Commandant Cousteaus can feast their eyes on a treasure trove of ocean finds.

Nice to Cannes

In all respects, this is one of the richest areas of the Côte d'Azur. The scenery can be absolutely magnificent, and art works abound both along the coast and in the villages of the hinterland.

ANTIBES AND JUAN-LES-PINS

Founded by the Phocaeans in the 4th century BC, **Antibes** got its name (Antipolis – the 'city opposite') because it lay facing Nice across the Baie des Anges. The first landmark you'll see here is the imposing square fortress, **Fort Carré**. This was the French kings' stronghold against the dukes of Savoy who controlled Nice. In 1794, Napoleon lodged his family here while supervising the coastal defence. Since he wasn't very well paid, his sisters filched figs and artichokes from neighbouring farmers. Today the hills around Antibes are lined with glassy greenhouses; growing flowers is the main local industry.

Don't miss a tour around the ramparts, rebuilt by Louis XIV's chief engineer, Vauban, in the 17th century along the original medieval lines.

South of the harbour, the Château Grimaldi, now **Musée Picasso**, is a white stone castle with a Romanesque tower built by the lords of Antibes on a Roman site. Besides several classical relics, the museum possesses a rich Picasso collection. In 1946, when the artist was having difficulty finding a place to work, the director of Antibes' museum offered him the premises as a studio. Picasso set to work among the dusty antiquities. Inspired by his surroundings, he completed over 145 works in a period of six months. The grateful artist donated these drawings, ceramics and paintings to the museum (see p.60).

Next to the château-museum is a 17th-century **church**

Indulge in a spot of dolce farniente. Antibes' beach is as laid back as its harbour is busy.

with a Romanesque apse and transept and an altarpiece attributed to Louis Bréa. Behind the sunny square you'll find a maze of old streets and the covered market, most colourful in the morning.

Just around the bay lies the **Cap d'Antibes**, a quiet, pine-covered peninsula, endowed with a wealth of big, beautiful houses and a venerable hotel, the Eden-Roc. It served as a model for F Scott Fitzgerald, and today you can usually see film stars and magnates lolling

around its pool poised high above the sea.

The **Chapelle Notre-Dame-du-Bon-Port** at **La Garoupe** is of curious composition: one

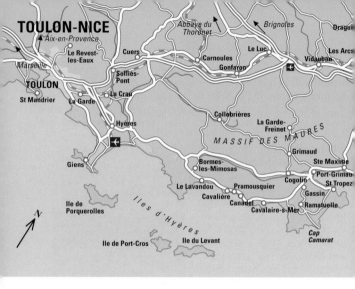

nave is 13th century, the other 16th and each is dedicated to a different madonna. They are both filled with *ex votos*, all kinds of naïve art works or objects offered as prayers of thanks to the Madonna.

Around the western side of the cape is the sandy crescent-shaped bay of **Juan-les-Pins**. The resort enjoyed its heyday in the 1920s and 1930s after American tycoon Frank Jay Gould built a big hotel and casino in a pinewood setting. Sleepy in winter, the town becomes rather wild in summer

with a gaudy atmosphere generated by a host of nightclubs, cafés, boutiques spilling their wares onto the streets and a restless, funseeking crowd of young people.

VALLAURIS AND BIOT

The artisans' towns of Vallauris and Biot are only a few minutes' drive from Antibes. **Vallauris** is inevitably associated with Picasso, who worked here after the war, and has given new impetus to a dying ceramics and pottery industry.

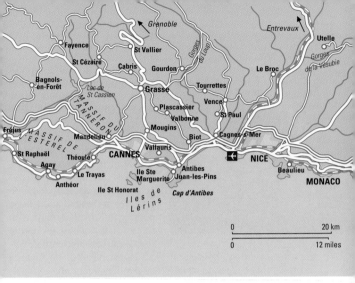

He presented the town with the bronze statue – *L'homme au mouton* (*Man with a Sheep*) – on Place Paul-Isnard, and decorated the Romanesque chapel there, now the Musée National 'La Guerre et la Paix' (National War and Peace Museum, also known as the Picasso Museum), with the murals *War and Peace*. Careful buyers still find worthwhile purchases in the ceramics shops that line Vallauris' one main street.

Perched on a cone-shaped hill, **Biot** also bulges with artisans' shops and has a restored Romanesque church (too dark most of the time to see a fine Bréa altarpiece) and a colourful 13th-century square with fountains and arcades.

Downhill, in the Biot glassworks, you can see craftsmen fashioning the heavy, tinted glass with minute bubbles for which the town is known.

Adjacent to Biot, the **Musée National Fernand Léger**, with its bold façade, stands out like a giant postage stamp from miles away. Light and airy inside, the modern structure, built and donated to France by **47**

the artist's widow, houses an incomparable collection of Léger's works – from paintings to huge tapestries (see p.60).

The dolphin show at Marineland, near the Biot railway station, is a hit with children, while food buffs will be interested in the Musée de l'Art Culinaire at **Villeneuve-Loubet**, the birthplace of chef Auguste Escoffier.

CAGNES-SUR-MER

Spread out over hills covered with orange and olive trees, **Cagnes-sur-Mer** is not one but three towns: the seaside resort of **Cros-de-Cagnes**, the modern commercial section of **Le Logis**, and the ancient hilltop fortress, **Haut-de-Cagnes** – the prettiest and most interesting part.

The narrow, cobbled streets corkscrew up to the **Castle Museum** (see p.60). To enter, you pass through an ivy-covered, oblique-angled patio with galleries all around and a huge pepper tree in the centre. On the ground floor of the castle visit a curious museum devoted to the olive – its history, cultivation, literature – probably the greatest tribute ever paid to that fruit.

Upstairs you'll find exhibits of contemporary art and a ceremonial hall with a splendid 17th-century *trompe-l'œil* ceiling, *The Fall of Phaeton*. One extraordinary room contains 40 portraits of Suzy Solidor, the one-time cabaret queen, as seen by famous 20th-century painters – ranging from a doe-eyed girl wearing a sailor suit by Van Dongen to a raffish, much older version of her wearing a matador's hat.

Auguste Renoir spent his last years (1907-19) in his villa, **Les Collettes**, just east of Cagnes. There's not much left to see here besides a few mementoes and a couple of the master's minor works, but the garden is lovely.

SAINT-PAUL-DE-VENCE

This is another venerable bastion, built within spade-shaped walls and looming over what were once green terraces of vineyards and cypress trees – now a parade of elegant country villas in lush gardens.

The walled feudal city, entered by foot under a tower and arch with a cannon pointing right at you, was built by Francis I in the 16th century as a defence against Nice and the dukes of Savoy.

Under the big plane trees of the Place du Général-de-Gaulle, you'll usually find a lively game of *pétanque* (or *boules*), the outdoor bowling game. The Colombe d'Or hotel across the street has an important private collection of modern art, acquired from Picasso, Léger and Calder in exchange for meals in the restaurant.

A tour of the narrow pedestrian streets takes only a few minutes, but take the time to stop at the Grande Fontaine and Gothic church.

On a wooded hill just outside Saint-Paul is one of the

*F*ind a shady street in delightful Haut-de-Cagnes (below), or relax among Picasso's works at the Château Grimaldi (left).

great modern art museums of the world – the **Fondation Maeght**, inaugurated in 1964 by art dealer Aimé Maeght and his wife. The museum sits in a green grove of dark pines. Full of visual surprises, the brick, steel and glass construction designed by Spanish-American architect José Luis Sert is an ideal place for displaying modern art. The permanent collection, including paintings and lithographs by many of the great names of 20th-century art, is packed away in summer to make room for a temporary show. Throughout the year you can see the superb sculpture collection, featuring many fine works by Miró and Giacometti (see p.60).

VENCE

Vence is an ancient bishopric with middle-age spread, as the charming old city has been girdled by newer shops and houses. English and French artists and retired people all like the bustling atmosphere, the surrounding hills and the peace that falls at night (off-season, of course).

In the 17th century, Antoine Godeau became Bishop of Vence. A misshapen society wit, he turned to holy orders at the age of 30, then undertook the restoration of the cathedral, founded new industries to give work to his parishioners and was appointed one of the first

Life imitating art? Chagall is just one of the painters represented at the Fondation Maeght.

members of the august Académie Française.

The best scenic points of old Vence are the **Place du Peyra** with its gurgling fountain and friendly cafés, the cathedral (particularly the arresting Romanesque belfry), and the **Place du Frêne** with a venerable ash tree whose trunk must be at least 2m (6ft) in diameter.

Tourists too often hurry past Vence on their way to the **Chapelle du Rosaire-Henri-Matisse** on the road to Saint-Jeannet (open to the public on certain days only; for opening times tel. 93.58.03.26). Dedicated by Matisse to the Dominican nuns who cared for him during a long illness, the chapel is the crowning achievement of the artist who was in his eighties and practically blind when he completed it. The stained-glass windows in bold patterns of royal blue, bright green and yellow give radiant light to the simple chapel, two walls of which are decorated by powerful line-drawing figures on white faience.

A short tour of the **Loup Valley** is worthwhile and will take you less than a day. Highlights include **Tourettes**, a delightful old town popular with artisans and artists, several waterfalls (Cascade de Courmes, Cascade des Demoiselles) and the town of **Gourdon**, built on a spur 758m (2,500ft) high. The castle here was a Saracen fort in the 9th century and contains a medieval museum.

GRASSE

Grasse, the perfume capital of the world, won't knock you over with heady scents, but you can't miss the enormous signs inviting you to visit the factories. Although the Grassois were distilling essential essences from local flowers as far back as the 13th century, the industry didn't bloom until the Italian Medici family launched the fashion of scented gloves in the 16th century (Grasse made gloves as well).

Nowadays the manufacturers use at least 10,000 tonnes of flowers – violets (from January to March), mimosa (February), daffodil (April), rose, orange-flowers and so on – in **51** order to produce their essence. The gleaming brass cauldrons, alembics and other trappings displayed in the factories, although mainly for show, do give an idea of the first steps in making perfume and soap.

The high price of perfume becomes understandable when you realize it takes a tonne of petals to produce just 1kg (2lb) of essence. The attractive soaps and scents on sale here have

From delicate flower arrangements to the massive Abbaye du Thoronet (right), Grasse and its hinterland offer varied contrasts.

very little to do with the sophisticated Paris-made brands, which use the Grasse essences in carefully guarded formulas.

Built on a steep hill, Grasse was already renowned for its clean air in the 19th century, and invalids and holiday-makers flocked here. The most charming spot in town is the friendly, crowded **Place aux Aires**, with its fountains, arcades and sculptured 18th-century façades. The morning market is a palette of colours (flowers and vegetables) under the blue shade of lotus (*micocoulier*) and plane trees.

A few blocks downhill, the Place aux Herbes has an even larger food market. Further on still is the sober, ochrestone **cathedral**, begun in the 12th century and restored in the 17th. Inside you'll find cradlevaulting and a rare religious canvas by Honoré Fragonard, *Le Lavement des Pieds* (*The Washing of the Feet*).

The **Villa-Musée Fragonard**, on the Boulevard Fragonard, occupies the villa where the artist spent a year during the French Revolution. He ar-

rived with a series of paintings depicting love scenes, which had been turned down in Paris by Madame du Barry. Most of the collection has ended up in the Frick Museum in New York, but the excellent and sensuous **Les Trois Grâces** (*Three Graces*) remains.

The **Musée d'Art et d'Histoire de Provence** in the Rue Mirabeau is housed in an elegant 18th-century town house once owned by the Marquise de Cabris (see p.60). The original furniture is in remarkably good condition, and among the less conventional and intriguing items on display, look out for a pewter bathtub on wheels and a carved wooden bidet-chair with a shell-shaped basin (see p.60).

CONTINUING INLAND

Grasse is a good starting point for delightful side trips. Gourdon and the Loup Valley (see p.51) are off to the north-east; to the south-west are the Tanneron range and the man-made lake of Saint-Cassien, a popular place for windsurfing.

Cabris (6km or 4 miles from Grasse on the D4 road) commands an impressive view from its old château ruins – the Tanneron hills, the Esterel and La Napoule to the right, Mougins and the Lérins Islands to the left; and on a clear day you can even make out the hazy outline of Corsica.

Another 8km (5 miles) or so further, the **Grottes de Saint-Cézaire** provide a refreshing respite from the sun, with stalactite shapes in extraordinary dark-red and pink colours.

As for **Saint-Cézaire** itself, it's a quiet, pretty town with a Romanesque chapel and a good view. You can continue north through wild, rocky limestone hills with low trees and bushes, up to **Mons** (32km or 20 miles from Grasse), an ancient perched village, to the **Col de Valferrière**, and back down the Route Napoléon through **Saint-Vallier** and some splendid panoramas.

Or you may want to continue west into the Var, visiting towns like **Fayence** (27km or 17 miles from Grasse), **Bargemon** (44km or 27½ miles) and **Draguignan** (some 56km or 35 miles away) or perhaps the **Abbaye du Thoronet** (a two-hour drive from Grasse). Lost in a beautiful landscape of reddish bauxite and green pine scrub trees, it's a cool, quiet place. The pink-stoned Thoronet, one of the three great abbeys of Provence, dates from the 12th century. It is notable for its clean-lined simplicity, its squat, colonnaded cloister and a hexagonal fountain, the *lavabo*, where the monks used to bathe.

Cannes

Pop. 68,000

During the film festival in May and the record fair (MIDEM) in January, Cannes loses its habitual cool. The rest of the year the city devotes itself to its touristic vocation – as an elegant, cosmopolitan resort in a splendid setting, boasting the liveliest pleasure port on the Côte d'Azur.

The history of Cannes is tied to the two islands you can see off the coast, the Lérins. On the smaller one, Saint Honorat founded a monastery in the 4th century which became a famous shrine for pilgrims. In the 10th century the Count of Antibes gave the Cannes mainland to the Lérins monks, who built ramparts to defend their territory against incursions by Moorish pirates.

By 1788, only four monks remained; the monastery was closed down and Cannes came under French rule. In 1815, Napoleon Bonaparte stopped there after landing at Golfe-Juan, but Cannes gave him such a chilly reception that he had to move on to Grasse.

A suitably imposing façade marks the entrance to one of La Croisette's most glamorous hotels.

Cannes is 'Discovered'

Cannes was just a quiet fishing village in 1834 when Lord Brougham, a leading English law reformer, had to stop over on his way to Italy because of a cholera epidemic. This chance visit turned out to be longer than expected: he built a home and returned every winter for the rest of his life. A champion of his city, Lord Brougham prodded King Louis Philippe to provide funds for a jetty below the old town. Many English aristocrats followed Brougham to Cannes, swelling the local population. A handsome statue of Lord Brougham presides over Prosper Mérimée Square, across from the Palais des Festivals.

LA CROISETTE

Like Nice's Promenade des Anglais, La Croisette is a magnificent showcase with gleaming hotels lining a flowered boulevard. The golden sand of the beach along the promenade is mainly imported from Fréjus. At one end of La Croisette lies the old port and the new **Palais des Festivals**; at the other, a second port and the Palm Beach Casino. The film festival, plus numerous other festivities, are held in the grand new Palais, which contains a casino as well.

Just a few blocks behind La Croisette is the Rue d'Antibes, one of the coast's most glamorous shopping streets. For more down-to-earth purchases – like T-shirts, sandals, mouth-

watering sausages and pastries – head for Rue Meynadier.

THE OLD TOWN

Looking uphill from the old port in the evening, you have a vision of the ramparts of the old town, **Le Suquet**, glowing with orange lights against the dark purple sky. You'll also see the **Tour du Suquet**, a 22m

(72ft) high square watchtower built by the Lérins monks. It was destroyed during the Revolution, but later restored, as a favour to local fishermen who petitioned for a tall, visible navigational point. Now the white stone clock-tower is a Cannes trademark.

The centre of the old town is Place de la Castre (from the Latin word for castle), a quiet, pine-shaded square. The 17th-century 'Gothic' church here, rather dim inside, has several polychrome statues. The **Musée de la Castre** (open from

The majestic sweep of Cannes' coastline attracts sun-worshippers and stars in equal numbers. **57**

These fortifications on the isle of Saint Honorat protected a most peaceful community of monks.

Lycklama, who is portrayed wearing an extraordinary oriental outfit.

The view over Cannes from Le Suquet is superb. For an even more spectacular panorama, go to the **observatory** at Super-Cannes.

ILES DE LÉRINS

One of Cannes' most refreshing diversions is an excursion to the islands. Boats leave frequently in the summer from the *Gare Maritime*: the trip to Sainte-Marguerite takes about 15 minutes; to Saint-Honorat, about 30 minutes. In season, the islands stage sound-and-light shows.

Closer to Cannes and largest of the islands is **Sainte-Marguerite**, consisting of 2.5km (1½ miles) of wooded hills, a minute 'main' street lined with fishermen's houses and a couple of restaurants. The island is named after Saint Honorat's sister, who founded her own religious order here.

You can walk for hours here among cool, fragrant woods and a grove of enormous euca-

10am to noon and 2 to 5pm, and 3 to 7pm from July to September; closed on Tuesday and throughout January) houses a quaintly eclectic collection of everything from an Egyptian mummy's hand to a Japanese warrior's costume and a South Pacific hut pole. The Persian objects are quite good. All this **58** is the gift of Dutchman Baron

lyptus trees – a Côte d'Azur staple that was first brought to the coast from Australia in the early 19th century.

Walk uphill to visit the old **Fort Royal**, built under Cardinal Richelieu, and enjoy a superb view of Cannes, Antibes and the hills. The main attraction here is the dank and smelly prison of the 'Man in the Iron Mask', whose identity has been hotly contested.

Between 1687 and 1698, a mysterious prisoner was kept here. He wore a mask of cloth, and not iron, but was never allowed to take it off – and nobody knows for sure who he was or why he was imprisoned. One theory identifies him as an illegitimate brother of Louis XIV; another as the larcenous ex-Finance minister of the Sun-King, Fouquet. There's nothing to see but chains, faded ochre stone and modern graffiti, but the legend is intriguing.

The island of **Saint-Honorat**, home of the monks who governed Cannes for nearly eight centuries, is once again a monastery, run by the Cistercian Order. Bright green, with umbrella pines, roses, lavender and the monks' vineyard, it's a peaceful retreat off-season. Several Romanesque barrel-vaulted chapels are scattered about.

The most striking construction on Saint-Honorat is the square, battlemented **Château** – really a fortified dungeon. Built in the 11th century over a Roman cistern, it served as a refuge for the monks during various attacks.

The 19th-century monastery is only open for special visits on request, but you can see the small museum and church, accompanied by a guide. Next door to the museum the monks do a brisk trade in handicrafts, lavender scent and their own liqueur – a redoubtable-looking, yellowish liquid.

AROUND CANNES

The coast's most glorious oddity, the **Château de la Napoule** (8km or 5 miles west of Cannes), hovers in red-rock splendour over a tiny beach and harbour. Here, in 1919, American sculptor Henry Clews (scion of a New York banking **59**

MUSEUM AND ART GALLERY HIGHLIGHTS

Usual opening hours are 9 or 10am to noon, and 2 to 6pm in winter; often later in the evening in summer.

Antibes. *Château Grimaldi-Musée Picasso, place du Château; tel. 92.90.54.20.* Classical relics plus an important Picasso collection. Closed Nov, Tues and Nat'l Holidays. Entrance fee: 25F. (See p.44)

Biot. *Musée Fernand-Léger; tel. 93.65.63.61.* Important collection of gigantic paintings and sculptures. Entrance fee: 35F. (See p.47)

Cagnes-sur-Mer. *Château, Haut-de-Cagnes; tel. 93.20.85.57.* Olive museum and modern art gallery. Closed Tues, Oct and Nat'l Holidays. Entrance fee: 5F. (See p.48)

Grasse. *Musée d'Art et d'Histoire de Provence, 2, rue Mirabeau; tel. 93.36.80.20.* Fine collection of art and traditions from eastern Provence. Closed Mon and Tues. (See p.53)
Villa-Musée Fragonard, boulevard Fragonard; tel. 93.36.01.61. Paintings plus furnishings and china. Closed Mon and Tues. Entrance fee: 10F. Free Sun and Wed. (See p.52)

Monaco. *Musée Océanographique; tel. 93.15.36.00.* Spectacular! Entrance fee: 60F, children 30F. (See p.42)

Nice. *Musée Matisse, av. des Arènes, Cimiez; tel. 93.81.08.08.* The artist's studio and an important exhibition of works. Closed Tues. Entrance free. (See p.26)
Musée d'Archéologie, av. des Arènes, Cimiez; tel. 93.81.59.57. Roman remains from 2nd and 3rd centuries AD. Closed Sun morning, Mon and first two weeks in Nov. Entrance free. (See p.27)
Musée Marc-Chagall, av. Docteur-Ménard; tel. 93.81.75.75. Permanent exhibition of 27 large-format biblical paintings. Closed Tues and 1 May. Entrance fee: 27F. (See p.26)

Saint-Tropez. *Musée de l'Annonciade, Le Port; tel. 94.97.04.01.* Late 19th- and early 20th-century paintings in a 16th-century chapel. Closed Tues and throughout Nov. Entrance fee: 22F. (See p.82)

Saint-Paul-de-Vence. *Fondation Maeght; tel. 93.32.81.63.* Great collection of modern art. Entrance fee: 40F. (See p.50)

family) restored the medieval château with towers and battlements, endowing every possible inch with his own work. Wildly imaginative, the sculptures range from a poignant Don Quixote to some pudgy grotesques.

The rather eccentric Clews, who saw himself as a latter-day Quixote and his wife as 'The Virgin of La Mancha', filled his home with all kinds of mottoes, ridiculing the 'aberrations' of society.

The museum can be visited by guided tour only, held twice daily at 3 and 4pm (plus 5pm in summer) except on a Tuesday from the months of February to November.

A soft and subtle backdrop of green hills characterizes the countryside between Cannes and Grasse. Interesting stops include **Mougins**, a 15th-century fortified town (with some superb restaurants, see pp.77-78); **Valbonne**, with its beautiful arcaded square shaded by big elm trees and a brightly restored Romanesque church; and **Plascassier**, a sleepy village perched on a hill.

The Esterel

Between Cannes and Saint-Raphaël lies a mass of porphyry rocks worn down and chipped by streams. This is the Esterel, now not much more than 600m (2,000ft) at its highest (Mt Vinaigre), though the landscape seems abrupt and impressive. In spring, however, the scrub-herb hills are softened by the golden hue of mimosa.

The original inland road here was the Aurelian Way, built by the eponymous Roman emperor in the 3rd century, but these days most people take the motorway running between Cannes and Saint-Raphaël.

There are excellent possibilities for exploring this area by foot or bike; further information can be obtained from the Conseil général du Var, 4, rue d'Antrechaus, 83000 Toulon; tel. 94.89.14.44.

THE GOLDEN CORNICHE

The motorway may be practical, but the coastal route – the Corniche d'Or (the Golden Corniche) – is much prettier. **61**

Red porphyry rocks tumble into the dark blue sea, making a jigsaw pattern of colours and shapes, tempting you to stop at every outcrop to admire the view or take a picture.

After **La Napoule** and then **Théoule**, with its château that served as a soap factory in the

A photo opportunity not to be missed: the golden rocks of the Esterel and the deep blue sea.

18th century, you come to **Port-la-Galère**, a cascade of modern houses on a flowered stony point. The Esterel is full of little resort towns with such euphonic names as **Le Trayas**, **Anthéor**, and **Agay** – an unpretentious resort. The Séma-phore du Dramont, built on the ruins of a watch-tower, offers sweeping views of the coast, and near the road is a marble monument commemorating the American landing here on 15 August 1944.

The best time to see this stretch of coastline is at sunset looking east, when colours and contrasts are most flamboyant – a surrealist's dream.

SAINT-RAPHAËL

Booming **Saint-Raphaël**, an appealing resort built around a port for pleasure boats, acts as a focus for the whole Esterel area. The town's **centre** is a pleasant, palm-lined modern sea-front (the old one was destroyed during World War II) with an ornamental fountain and pyramid commemorating Napoleon Bonaparte's debarkation after the 1799 Egyptian victories (see p.16).

In days gone by, there was a small holiday resort here for Roman legions based in nearby Fréjus. It stood more or less on the site of the present **casino** – if you can imagine the roulette tables replaced by tile baths and fish ponds.

The 12th-century **Templars' church** in the old town (Rue des Templiers) is surmounted with a massive watch-tower replacing the right-hand apse.

FRÉJUS

Little remains of the busy Roman market town of Fréjus (Forum Julii) founded in 49BC. The big harbour, built by Emperor Augustus into a great naval base and shipyard, has been completely filled up with silt deposits and replaced by modern Fréjus. A good part of the town was also rebuilt after the 1959 catastrophe, when a dam upstream over the River Reyran broke, killing over 400 people. At the mouth of the river a new marina and apartment complex is now nearing completion.

Most impressive of Fréjus' Roman vestiges is the **Arènes** (arena), a restored grey-green construction which could seat 10,000 spectators – nearly as large as the arenas of Arles and Nîmes. It is closed on Tuesday. During the season, bullfights are held here.

Other Roman ruins include a theatre and the massive reddish arches of the aqueduct that brought water in from the River Siagnole.

Nearly destroyed by the Saracens in the 10th century, the **63** town was revived in 990 by Bishop Riculphe, who established a fortified **episcopal city** here with a cathedral, baptistery, cloister and bishop's palace. Put your name down for a guided tour to see the carved Renaissance doors, the baptistery and the cloisters.

One of the oldest religious buildings in France (late 4th to early 5th century), the octagonal **baptistery** is punctuated by handsome black granite columns with Corinthian capitals (from the ancient Fréjus forum). The terracotta baptismal bowl, the original, was discovered in the course of archaeological research.

In the **cloister**, a double-deckered arcade surrounds a sweet-smelling garden of roses and cypress trees. The ceiling of the upstairs arcade is decorated with some amusing 14th-century creatures – imaginative scenes from the Apocalypse. An archaeological museum adjoining the cloister has Gallo-Roman remains.

As for the 10th- to 12th-century **cathedral** (closed Tuesday), with its 'broken cradle' vaulting, it perfectly exemplifies the early Gothic style of the region. It was built on the site of a Roman temple dedicated to Jupiter.

Today peaceful and unassuming, Fréjus was once a bustling Roman market town.

A Selection of Recommended Hotels and Restaurants on the Côte d'Azur

Recommended Hotels

The Côte d'Azur is a popular destination, and the tourist infrastructure is accordingly vast and efficient, with a large number of establishments catering to all tastes. In high season, however, accommodation can be difficult to find, and you are advised to book well in advance.

Our selection is based on geographical location and quality of accommodation. (Some of the restaurants listed on pp.74-80 also have rooms.) To give you an indication of price, we have used the symbols below for the average cost of a double room per night, in season, excluding breakfast (all rooms with private bath or shower). Prices may vary slightly out of season.

ⅠⅠⅠ	over 800F
ⅠⅠ	400-800F
Ⅰ	under 400F

ANTIBES

Bleu Marine   Ⅰ
rue des 4 chemins, 06600 Antibes
Tel. 93.74.84.84
Fax 93.95.90.26
Simple modern hotel, 500m from the beach. All bedrooms have sea views. Lift and private parking. No restaurant. 18 bedrooms.

Mas Djoliba   ⅠⅠ
29, avenue de Provence
06600 Antibes
Tel. 93.34.02.48; fax 93.34.05.81
Pretty, Provençal-style hotel, well situated within walking distance of both the old town and beach. Gardens, swimming pool. Dinner available for house guests only. Private parking. 14 bedrooms.

BEAULIEU-sur-MER

Le Métropole   ⅠⅠⅠ
boulevard du Général-Leclerc
06310 Beaulieu-sur-Mer
Tel. 93.01.00.08
Fax 93.01.18.51
A grand hotel retaining echoes of the Côte d'Azur's heyday, in an idyllic setting. Private beach offering all sea sports and a heated pool. Beautifully appointed rooms and suites, many with uninterrupted sea views. Excellent restaurant serving *haute cuisine*, closed Monday. 50 bedrooms and suites.

CAGNES-sur-MER

Les Collettes ▯
38, chemin des Collettes
06800 Cagnes-sur-Mer
Tel. 93.20.80.66
Delightful small hotel with garden, swimming pool and tennis court, in a quiet street. Most rooms with sea view; some with kitchenette. Parking. No restaurant. Reserve. 13 bedrooms.

CANNES

Carlton Intercontinental ▯▯▯
58, La Croisette
06400 Cannes
Tel. 93.68.91.68
Fax 93.38.20.90
Prestigious hotel with superb, luxurious bedrooms and apartments. Elegant *belle époque* architecture, private beach, health club, swimming pool, conference facilities, private parking. Highly rated restaurants, La Belle Otéro and La Côte. 325 rooms; 30 apartments.

Hôtel de Paris ▯▯
34, boulevard d'Alsace
06400 Cannes
Tel. 93.38.30.89
Fax 93.39.04.61
Classic, turn-of-the-century *belle époque* architecture, in the centre of Cannes but with a private beach 30m away. Garden, shaded swimming pool. Very comfortable bedrooms and luxurious suites, all with sound-proofing and air-conditioning. No restaurant, but the hotel has dinner arrangements with various nearby restaurants. Conference facilities. Garage parking. Closed mid-November to mid-December. 45 bedrooms; 5 suites.

Hôtel Select ▯
16, rue Hélène-Vagliano
06400 Cannes
Tel. 93.99.51.00
Fax 93.98.03.12
Reasonably priced and very central (only 200m from La Croisette). Well-equipped bedrooms with double-glazing and air-conditioning. No restaurant. Public car park opposite. 30 bedrooms.

Ruc Hôtel ▯▯
15, boulevard de Strasbourg
06400 Cannes
Tel. 93.38.64.32
Fax 93.39.54.18
Elegant hotel with beautiful 18th-century furnishings. Well-decorated bedrooms, some of which open onto a courtyard garden. Top-floor terrace has views over the hills. Tennis club and swimming pool next door. Secured public parking nearby. No restaurant. 30 rooms. **67**

CAVALIÈRE

Le Club ▮▮▮
plage de Cavalière
83980 Cavalière
Tel. 94.05.80.14
Fax 79.08.58.38
Holiday complex comprising spacious bedrooms and a few apartments and a few apartments on a sandy private beach. Choice of sea sports; swimming pool, tennis courts and gardens. Conference facilities. Open May-October. 28 rooms; 4 apartments.

EZE

Château Eza ▮▮▮
06360 Eze
Tel. 93.41.12.24
Fax 93.41.16.64
Just a few exceptional bedrooms in this restaurant, with rooms created from a group of medieval houses. Acclaimed restaurant. No vehicular access. Open Easter-Oct. Five bedrooms; three apartments.

GRIMAUD

La Boulangerie ▮▮
route de Collobrières
83310 Grimaud
Tel. 94.43.23.16
Fax 94.43.38.27
Quiet situation, just 5km (3 miles) from the coast, this friendy and in-

formal Provençal hotel has charming bedrooms and gardens with swimming pool and tennis court. Fine views over the Maures mountains and a restaurant serving lunch only for residents. Open April-October. 11 bedrooms.

HYÈRES

Auberge ▮▮-▮▮▮
Les Glycines
Ile de Porquerolles
83400 Hyères
Tel. 94.58.30.36
Fax 94.58.35.22
Access to the island is by ferry or *bateau-taxi* from Hyères, Cavalaire or Toulon (cars are not allowed on the island). Provençal inn set in pretty gardens, overlooking the village square. Air-conditioned bedrooms and a restaurant specializing in local cuisine with plenty of seafood. Open April-October. 17 bedrooms.

JUAN-les-PINS

Belles Rives ▮▮▮
boulevard du Littoral
06160 Juan-les-Pins
Tel. 93.61.02.79
Fax 93.67.43.51
Retaining its original air of luxury from the 1930s and situated right on the beach with views over Cap

d'Antibes. Air-conditioned bedrooms, swimming pool and all sea sports. Conference facilities. The restaurant with a terrace at the water's edge offers the ultimate in romantic wining and dining. Open April-October. 41 bedrooms.

Les Mimosas ▮▮
rue Pauline
06160 Juan-les-Pins
Tel. 93.61.04.16
Fax 92.93.06.46
A hotel situated in quiet gardens with swimming pool, 5 minutes' walk from the beach. Attractive bedrooms with terrace. No restaurant. Private parking. Open May-September. 34 bedrooms.

MENTON

L'Aiglon ▮▮
7, avenue Madone
06500 Menton
Tel. 93.57.55.55
Fax 93.35.92.39
An attractive 19th-century hotel with private gardens and a heated swimming pool. Located close to the beach and within easy walking distance of the town centre. Spacious, well-equipped bedrooms and suites. Reasonably priced restaurant Le Riaumont. Parking. Closed mid-November to mid-December. 30 bedrooms and suites.

MONACO

Monte Carlo Beach Hotel ▮▮▮
06190 Roquebrune-Cap-Martin
Tel. 93.28.66.66
Fax 93.78.14.18
In an idyllic headland setting just outside Monaco, this luxurious seaside holiday resort hotel has an olympic-sized swimming pool and glamorous canvas bathing tents all along the perfect beach. Air-conditioned bedrooms, each with a balcony overlooking the sea. Restaurant La Virgie serves a sumptuous buffet every lunchtime and candle-lit dinners at night. Open March-October. 44 rooms.

MOUGINS

Le Manoir de l'Etang ▮▮
66, allée du Manoir
06250 Mougins
Tel. 93.90.01.07
Fax 92.92.20.70
Set 2km (1¼ miles) outside town and very peaceful, this lovely 19th-century house has tastefully decorated bedrooms and a restaurant offering refined cuisine. Glorious Provençal garden with swimming pool. Parking. Closed November and February. Restaurant closed Sunday evening and Monday except in high season. 15 bedrooms. **69**

NICE

Les Cigognes

16, rue Maccarani
06000 Nice
Tel. 93.88.65.02
Fantastic value in this three-star rated hotel conveniently sited between the station and the Promenade des Anglais. Reception with period furnishings. Lift. Budget-priced breakfast. No restaurant. 30 bedrooms.

Grand Hôtel Aston

12, avenue Félix-Faure
06000 Nice
Tel. 93.80.62.52
Fax 93.80.40.02
Very central – facing Place Masséna – and a few minutes' walk from the beach. Air-conditioned bedrooms. Roof-top garden and terrace with sea views. Restaurant. Conference facilities. Parking nearby. 160 bedrooms and suites.

Negresco

37, promenade des Anglais
06000 Nice
Tel. 93.88.39.51
Fax 93.88.35.68
One of the world's great hotels, built in 1912 and marvellously situated on the promenade. Flamboyant *belle époque* architecture with distinctive domed turrets. Magnificent bedrooms and apartments furnished with antiques. The celebrated Chantecler restaurant is acknowledged as one of the best (and ultra-expensive) tables of the region (closed mid-November to mid-December). La Rotonde is a less formal brasserie, serving until midnight. Valet parking. 150 bedrooms and apartments.

La Pérouse

11, quai Rauba-Capeu
06000 Nice
Tel. 93.62.34.63
Fax 93.62.59.41
Remarkable hotel in an amazing semi-suspended situation. Set in gardens with lemon trees beneath the château, access is via two lifts from the quayside. Modern Mediterranean architecture and stunning views over the Baie des Anges. Air-conditioned rooms, some with a terrace. Swimming pool. Restaurant specializing in alfresco grills (May-September). 65 bedrooms.

Windsor

11, rue Dalpozzo
06000 Nice
Tel. 93.88.59.35
Fax 93.88.94.57
Interesting city-centre hotel completely renovated. Comfortable bedrooms, most air-conditioned, some with balconies. No restau-

rant but light meals served in the bar. Tropical garden with swimming pool. Jacuzzi. Gymnasium. Lift. Parking. 60 bedrooms.

PLAN-de-la-TOUR

Mas des Brugassiers   ‖
83120 Plan-de-la-Tour
Tel. 94.43.72.42
Fax 94.43.00.20
Built in the 1970s in an attractive rustic Provençal style and peacefully situated 1.5km (1 mile) outside the village. The bedrooms are fresh and cool with traditional tiled floors, some opening onto the garden and swimming pool. No restaurant. Open March-October. 14 bedrooms.

RAMATUELLE

La Ferme d'Augustin   ‖‖
plage Tahiti
83350 Ramatuelle
Tel. 94.97.23.83
Fax 94.97.40.30
Set in vineyards and next to Tahiti Beach, this lovely old farmhouse is surrounded by luxuriant gardens. The bedrooms overlook the gardens and many have balconies and sea views. No restaurant but the bar serves snacks. Heated swimming pool. Secured parking. Open March-October. 45 bedrooms.

SAINT-JEAN-CAP-FERRAT

Brise Marine   ‖
58, avenue Jean-Mermoz
06230 Saint-Jean-Cap-Ferrat
Tel. 93.76.04.36
Fax 93.76.11.49
Fairly small but immaculate bedrooms in this authentic turn-of-the-century villa enjoying a privileged position overlooking the Mediterranean. A steeply terraced garden adorned with palm trees, fountains and flower pots leads down to the sea. No restaurant. Advance booking absolutely essential. Open February-October. 16 bedrooms.

SAINT-PAUL-DE-VENCE

Hôtel Le Hameau   ‖-‖
528, route de La Colle
06570 Saint-Paul-de-Vence
Tel. 93.32.80.24
Fax 93.25.55.75
Characterful 18th-century whitewashed farmhouse and outbuildings set in terraced orange and lemon groves just outside the town. Comfortable bedrooms and apartments attractively decorated in rustic Provençal style, some with a terrace. No restaurant. Parking. Closed from mid-November to mid-December. 14 bedrooms.

SAINT-RAPHAËL

Golf-Hôtel de Valescure   ▯▯

Golf de Valescure
83700 Saint-Raphaël
Tel. 94.82.40.31
Fax 94.82.41.88

On a sports and golf complex 5km (3 miles) outside town. Modern hotel with light, airy bedrooms. Gardens with swimming pool and tennis courts. Restaurant. Golf and tennis lessons available.

SAINT-TROPEZ

Les Capucines   ▯▯▯

domaine du Treizain
83990 Saint-Tropez
Tel. 94.97.70.05/06
Fax 94.47.55.85

Reasonably priced by local standards and set in pine woods outside the town. A modern complex of Provençal style houses provides 24 rooms, some with air-conditioning and private terraces. Swimming pool. Jacuzzi. No restaurant. Parking. Open March-October.

La Ponche   ▯▯-▯▯▯

place du Revelin
83990 Saint-Tropez
Tel. 94.97.02.53
Fax 94.97.78.61

Central but tucked away in a side street right next to the Port des Pêcheurs and created from a group of fishermen's cottages. Bedrooms vary greatly in size and price but are all stylish, some with private roof-top terraces and sea views. Lively, good-value restaurant with pavement terrace. Restaurant service until midnight. Open March-October. 20 bedrooms.

Lou Troupelen   ▯-▯▯

chemin des Vendanges
83990 Saint-Tropez
Tel. 94.97.44.88
Fax 94.97.41.76

Great value for money and only 1km (½ a mile) out of Saint-Tropez amongst the vineyards. Large Provençal house with garden. Some of the bedrooms have a terrace. Parking. Open April-October. 45 bedrooms.

Le Yaca   ▯▯▯

1, boulevard d'Aumale
83990 Saint-Tropez
Tel. 94.97.11.79
Fax 94.97.58.50

Very comfortable air-conditioned bedrooms in an elegant 200-year-old house situated in the old town between the port and the Citadelle. Some rooms with terrace overlooking the sea or the super garden with a swimming pool. No restaurant. Valet parking nearby. Open April-October. 22 bedrooms.

SAINTE-MAXIME

Hôtel de la Poste ⏸
7, boulevard Mistral
83120 Sainte-Maxime
Tel. 94.96.18.33
Fax 94.96.41.68
Right in the centre of town and a few minutes' walk to the beach. Elegant bedrooms and a secret courtyard with swimming pool. Open May-October. 24 bedrooms.

Marie-Louise ▯
Hameau Guerreville
83120 Sainte-Maxime
Tel. 94.96.06.05
A small family-run hotel in peaceful surroundings 2km (1¼ miles) out of town and 200m from the sea. Simple, pretty rooms, some with sea view. Home-cooking, with half-board obligatory in high season. Children welcome. Parking. Closed November. 14 bedrooms.

VENCE

Auberge des Seigneurs ▯
place du Frêne
06140 Vence
Tel. 93.58.02.24
Fax 93.24.08.01
In the oldest part of the old town, an atmospheric and historic inn dating back centuries but particularly associated with the painters –

Renoir, Modigliani, Dufy – who stayed here. Bedrooms are typically Provençal. Popular restaurant specializes in local cuisine. Closed first two weeks in July, mid-November to mid-December and Monday. 10 bedrooms.

Hôtel Diana ▯
avenue des Poilus
06140 Vence
Tel. 93.58.28.56
Fax 93.24.64.06
A modern, central hotel on the edge of the old town. Comfortable rooms, all with private terrace, some with kitchenette. No restaurant. Large public underground car park next door. Open all year except first two weeks in November. 25 bedrooms.

VILLEFRANCHE-sur-MER

Hôtel Welcome ⏸
1, quai Amiral Courbet
06230 Villefranche-sur-Mer
Tel. 93.76.76.93
Fax 93.01.88.81
Right on the colourful quayside and built fairly recently on the site of an old convent. Spacious, comfortable, air-conditioned rooms, most with balconies overlooking the port. Restaurant. Conference rooms. Closed mid-November to mid-December. 32 bedrooms.

73

Recommended Restaurants

The Côte d'Azur doesn't lack grand, renowned establishments, but you can dine equally well in the more humble restaurants. As a rule, the closer to the seafront the establishment, the more expensive the meal – so it pays to step back a little in the main towns and resorts, and to explore the hinterland.

The following list can only be selective. We have concentrated on the main tourist resorts, highlighting those restaurants combining high-quality food with great service. It is advisable to book in advance, especially in high season. Lunch is generally served between 12 noon and 2pm – sometimes later in the main resorts – and last orders for dinner are taken round 9pm in most rural areas. To give an indication of price range, we have used the following symbols for a three-course meal for one person, excluding wine. *Bon appétit!*

▌▌▌	over 250F
▌▌	150-250F
▌	under 150F

ANTIBES

L'Eléphant Bleu ▌
28, boulevard d'Aguillon
06600 Antibes
Tel. 93.34.28.80
An attractive ethnic restaurant specializing in Thai cuisine, set in the port area of Antibes. Open every day from lunchtime to 11.30pm.

Le Romantique ▌
5, rue Rostan
Tel. 93.34.59.39
Excellent Provençal cooking at very reasonable prices in a charming rustic restaurant in the heart of old Antibes. Closed Sunday evening plus Tuesday evening and Wednesday lunch in low season.

Les Vieux Murs ▌▌-▌▌▌
Avenue Amiral-de-Grasse
06600 Antibes
Tel. 93.34.06.73/93.34.66.73
Fax 93.34.81.08
Ever-popular establishment, perfectly placed on the ramparts of old Antibes. Accomplished cuisine from chef/owner Georges Romano and a good selection of regional wines. Valet parking.

BIOT

Galerie des Arcades   I-II
16, place des Arcades
06410 Biot
Tel. 93.65.01.04
Something of an institution! Popular 15th century-village inn, a favourite with artists in the 1960s, serves resolutely Provençal cuisine in a small dining room or outside under medieval arcades. 12 very individual bedrooms with antique furnishings (price range II).

CAGNES-sur-MER

Le Cagnard   III
rue Pontis-Long
06800 Haut-de-Cagnes
Tel. 93.20.73.21
Fax 93.20.06.39
Reputed restaurant serving sophisticated cuisine from Jean-Yves Johany. 28 elegant bedrooms and apartments, most with balconies (price range II - III). Closed mid-November to mid-December. Restaurant closed Thursday lunch.

Restaurant des Peintres   II
71, montée de la Bourgade
06800 Haut-de-Cagnes
Tel. 93.20.83.08
Fax 93.20.61.10
A lovely old house with a talented young chef. Refined cooking featuring the best of local ingredients. Weekday lunch menu offers great value. Closed Wednesday.

CANNES

Aux Bons Enfants   I
80, rue Meynadier
06400 Cannes
In a back street behind the port, a simple café serving excellent home cooking. No telephone. Closed at Christmas, Sunday evening plus Saturday evening in low season.

Caffé Roma   II
1, square Mérimée
06400 Cannes
Tel. 93.38.05.04
A chic and lively rendezvous opposite the Palais. Cocktails plus an Italian menu; relatively good value *plat du jour* (dish of the day) and excellent ice-creams. Terrace.

La Poêle d'Or   II
23, rue des Etats-Unis
06400 Cannes
Tel. 93.39.77.65
Fax 93.40.45.59
Just behind La Croisette. Consistently good classic cooking with an interesting choice of seafood dishes. Special monthly wine selection. Reservation essential at weekends. Closed Monday evening and all day Tuesday.

75

Royal Gray   ▮▮▮

Hôtel Gray Albion
6, rue des Etats-Unis
Tel. 92.99.79.79
Fax 93.99.26.10
Modern, light, inventive and highly regarded cuisine in contemporary setting. Good-value weekday lunch menu. Closed February and Monday lunch. 180 luxurious bedrooms and apartments (price range ▮▮▮). Private beach. Disco. Piano bar. Shopping mall. Parking.

GRIMAUD

Le Côteau Fleuri   ▮▮

place Pénitants, 83310 Grimaud
Tel. 94.43.20.17
Fax 94.43.33.42
Popular 18th-century hotel/restaurant, quietly situated. Renowned locally for above-average cooking. Welcoming atmosphere. Provençal décor. Terrace. 14 bedrooms (price range ▮-▮▮ depending on size). Closed mid-November to mid-December and Tuesday.

HYÈRES

La Colombe   ▮-▮▮

quartier de la Bayorre
83400 Hyères
Tel. 94.65.02.15
An attractive rustic restaurant with excellent, serious cooking by the young chef/owner – Pascal Bonomy. Seafood, Provence-inspired dishes and interesting local wines.

JUAN-LES-PINS

La Terrace   ▮▮▮

Hôtel Juana, La Pinède
avenue Georges-Gallice
Tel. 93.61.08.70
Fax 93.61.76.60
06160 Juan-les-Pins
One of the great restaurants on the Côte d'Azur, well known for its romantic associations with Scott Fitzgerald. Sophisticated and innovative modern cuisine. Lunch menu (except Sunday) offers remarkable value. Closed Wednesday except public holidays and in high summer. 45 luxurious bedrooms (price range ▮▮▮). Hotel and restaurant open April-Oct.

MONACO

Café de Paris   ▮▮▮

place du Casino
98000 Monaco
Tel. 93.50.57.75
Fax 93.25.46.98
A faithful re-creation of the original *belle époque* bar and brasserie, next door to the famous Casino. Pavement terrace plus a nostalgic restaurant with 1900s décor and dining terrace.

Louis XV ▮▮▮

Hôtel de Paris
place du Casino, 98000 Monaco
Tel. 92.16.30.01/92.10.30.06
Fax 92.16.69.21
Under master-chef Alain Ducasse, the Louis XV has become one of the most glamorous restaurants in Europe. Unashamedly sumptuous décor and immaculate service. The widely acclaimed cuisine takes Mediterranean cooking to the dizzy heights of *haute cuisine* and the wine cellar equals any in the world. Advance booking preferred. Closed Tuesday.

Polpetta ▮▮

2, rue Paradis
98000 Monaco
Tel. 93.50.67.84
Resolutely Italian trattoria, serving pasta and seafood dishes. Outside dining terrace. Animated and popular. Reserve. Closed Saturday lunch and all day Tuesday.

Restaurant Tony ▮

6, rue Comte-Félix-Gastaldi
98000 Monaco
Tel. 93.30.81.37
Fax 93.30.67.48
In the old town close to the Palace, a simple bistro offering good food at prices not easily found in Monaco. Closed Nov, Dec and Saturday out of high season.

Le Saint-Benoît ▮▮

10, terrasse avenue de la Costa
98000 Monaco
Tel. 93.25.02.34
Fax 93.30.52.64
Situated in a roof-top position by the old port with views over the Rock and the Royal Palace. Fine cuisine and lots of fish dishes. An interesting lunch menu including wine, daily except Sunday. Closed Monday and mid-Dec. to mid-Jan.

MOUGINS

Le Bistrot de Mougins ▮▮

place du Village, 06250 Mougins
Tel. 93.75.78.34
Fax 93.75.25.52
In the centre of Mougins, in the vaulted cellars of an old coaching inn. Modern Provence-inspired cooking. Popular and reasonably priced (by Mougins standards) so booking advised. Closed mid-November to mid-December.

Moulin de Mougins ▮▮▮

quartier Notre-Dame-de-Vie
06260 Mougins
Tel. 93.75.78.24
Fax 93.90.18.55
Master-chef Roger Vergé's world-renowned restaurant in a lovely old olive mill outside town. Mediterranean cooking at its most innovative in an enchanting setting. **77**

Excellent selection of the best local wines. Five luxurious bedrooms (price range ▮▮▮). Closed February, March and Monday lunch.

Les Muscadines ▮▮-▮▮▮

18, boulevard Courteline
06250 Mougins
Tel. 93.90.00.43
Fax 92.92.88.23

One of the best tables in Mougins. Beautifully decorated dining room with a terrace overlooking Cannes. An extensive choice of à la carte dishes and good value set menus. Eight elegant bedrooms (price range ▮▮). Closed February; Tuesday; and Wednesday lunch.

NICE

L'Ane Rouge ▮▮▮

7, quai Deux-Emmanuel
06000 Nice
Tel. 93.89.49.63

Best of the fish restaurants at the old port. Excellent selection of white wines. Terrace. Valet parking. Open Monday-Friday only. Closed mid-July to end of August.

Don Camillo ▮▮

5, rue des Ponchettes
06000 Nice
Tel. 93.85.67.95

A reputed restaurant just off Cours Selaya in old Nice, where chef Franck Cerutti's innovative adaptations of local dishes have won high acclaim. Good selection of Provençal wines. Closed Sunday.

L'Escalinada ▮

22, rue Pairolière
06000 Nice
Tel. 93.62.11.71

Genuine Niçoise cuisine in the heart of old Nice. Specialities include ravioli and gnocci plus the traditional *socca* – large pancake made from chickpea flour. Service until 11pm.

Grand Café de Turin ▮

5, place Garibaldi
06000 Nice
Tel. 93.62.29.52

Very popular seafood restaurant with tables under pavement arcades. Fresh oysters and shellfish on display. White wine by the jug. Always full of office workers at lunchtime.

La Méranda ▮▮

4, rue de la Terrasse
06000 Nice

Unique! Authentic Niçois bistro in the heart of old Nice, serving traditional local cuisine. No telephone. Orders taken until 9.30pm. Closed February, August, Saturday, Sunday and Monday. No credit cards accepted.

Les Préjugés du Palais ▌▌-▌▌▌

1, place du Palais
06000 Nice
Tel. 93.62.37.03

Busy restaurant in old Nice with a terrace for outside dining and people-watching. High quality classic cuisine with a set lunch menu offering great value for money. Closed from mid-October to mid-November and Sunday.

RAMATUELLE

Chez Camille ▌▌▌

quartier Bonne-Terrasse
83350 Ramatuelle
Tel. 94.79.80.38

Ultra-fashionable seafood restaurant on the beach 5km (3 miles) outside town. Good *bouillabaisse*. Advance booking almost essential at weekends and in high season. Open Apr-Sept. Closed Tuesday lunch except in high season.

SAINT-JEAN-CAP-FERRAT

Le Provençal ▌▌▌

2, avenue Denis-Semeria
06230 Saint-Jean-Cap-Ferrat
Tel. 93.76.03.97
Fax 93.76.05.39

Jean-Jaques Jouteux is one of the new culinary stars of the Côte d'Azur. Established in an attractive restaurant perched above the port of Saint-Jean, he offers a brilliant repertoire of Provence-inspired dishes plus a great value weekday lunch menu. Closed February and Monday in low season.

SAINT-PAUL-DE-VENCE

La Brouette ▌

830, route de Cagnes
06570 Saint-Paul-de-Vence
Tel. 93.58.67.16

A popular Danish-owned restaurant serving a selection of French dishes with plenty of typical Scandinavian specialities. Quality produce, generous portions and very reasonable prices. Located outside the town with good views over Saint-Paul. Closed February and Monday.

SAINT-RAPHAËL

Le Pastorel ▌▌

54, rue de la Liberté
83700 Saint-Raphaël
Tel. 94.95.02.36
Fax 94.95.64.07

Great value set menus in this charming old house with attractive vine-covered dining terrace. Many Provençal specialities including lots of seafood dishes and a superb **79** hors-d'œuvre table. Closed Sunday evening and all day Monday plus lunchtime in August.

SAINT-TROPEZ

L'Echalote   ‖
35, rue Général Allard
83990 Saint-Tropez
Tel. 94.54.83.26
Fax 94.54.34.94
Well-known restaurant taking its name from the house speciality – *bœuf à l'echalote*. Excellent meat dishes. Good value set menu including wine. Garden. Closed mid-November to mid-December.

Le Girelier   ‖
Le Port des Pêcheurs
83990 Saint-Tropez
Tel. 94.97.03.87
Fax 94.97.43.86
A popular and friendly quayside fish restaurant, with a typical marine décor. Outside dining in summer. Open March-October. Closed Wednesday.

SAINTE-MAXIME

L'Amiral   ‖
Le Port
83120 Sainte-Maxime
Tel. 94.43.99.36
An interesting menu with lots of seafood dishes in this pleasant restaurant overlooking the boating marina. Outside dining in summer. Closed mid-November to mid-December and Monday.

Hostellerie   ‖-‖
La Croisette
2, boulevard des Romarins
83120 Sainte-Maxime
Tel. 94.96.17.75
A pretty restaurant in a pink-tinted villa situated on the coast to the west of the main town. Refined, delicate cuisine with lots of seafood dishes. Garden and outside dining in summer. Open for dinner only. 17 attractive bedrooms with Provençal décor (price range ‖), some with terrace and sea views. Open February to November.

VENCE

La Farigoule   ‖
15, rue Henri-Isnard
06140 Vence
Tel. 93.58.01.27
Authentic Provençal home cooking by Madame Gastaud at prices that offer remarkable value. The restaurant takes its name from her speciality – *lapin à la farigoule* (rabbit stuffed with fresh thyme). Outside dining in summer. Closed mid-November to mid-December; Friday and Saturday lunch. No credit cards accepted.

Côte des Maures

The Côte des Maures is possibly the most exclusive stretch of the Côte d'Azur, culminating as it does with legendary Saint-Tropez. Inland, the Massif des Maures offers a welcome respite from the fray.

On the way to Saint-Tropez, you'll pass through the attractive town of **Sainte-Maxime**, with a casino, a minute beach and a wide promenade. This popular holiday resort, with its palm trees and esplanade, retains an appealing, almost Victorian atmosphere that is quite different to that of fashionable Saint-Tropez across the bay.

SAINT-TROPEZ

It barely manages to keep up with its glamorous reputation: celebrity escapades, the beauty of its little port, cafés filled with fashionable people, chic boutiques and casual nudity on nearby beaches.

Brigitte Bardot threatens to leave now, but other stars still come out at night to haunt the 'in' cafés and discothèques. In Saint-Tropez more than any other place on the Côte d'Azur, you feel an unspoken desire to wear the right T-shirt, be seen with the right people and show up in certain places at certain times of day or night. The atmosphere is enlivened by clusters of motorcycles roaring by, as well as haughty models and golden boys parading around. In winter it reverts back to that of an easy-going fishing town.

The resort weathers its own snobbery while cultivating its legends. The name comes from a Roman Christian, Torpes (an officer of the capricious Nero), who was martyred in Pisa in AD68. The headless body, put adrift in a boat with a dog and a cockerel, came ashore in the Var region. In the local church you can see a tableau of the body drifting along with its animal companion, as well as a wide-eyed sculpture of the saint himself, neatly mustachioed, surrounded with a lacy halo, his chest covered with heart-shaped medals.

The town was battered several times by the Saracens, and more recently by the German **81** occupation and invasions of World War II, but the gallant little fishing village always sprang back. In 1637 it routed a fleet of Spanish ships and still celebrates the victory in May with the **Bravade**, a fête that also honours Saint Tropez himself (see p.102). The natives get out their muskets, don 17th- and 18th-century costumes and fire blanks all over the place in fun, noisy parades. (There is a similar but less important festival in mid-June.)

Saint-Tropez was first 'discovered' by the French writer Guy de Maupassant; it became very fashionable in the 1920s, when it was visited and painted by Dunoyer de Segonzac, Dufy, Bonnard, and Signac; Colette wrote reams in her villa here, La Treille Muscate.

After World War II, the town managed to put itself together again, wisely rejecting plans for modern urban development.

The Port

You can't miss the **port** with its restless crowds, shiny yachts and pastel houses with red-tile roofs, most of them rebuilt in the old fishermen's style.

Nearby the plane-tree-shaded **Place des Lices** is full of local colour: a lively food market takes over several mornings a week, and *pétanque* (bowls) games are the centre of interest in the late afternoon.

The **Musée de l'Annonciade**, a former chapel situated on the west side of the port, houses an excellent collection of Impressionist and Post-Impressionist works (see p.60). Many of the artists lived in and loved Saint-Tropez. You can view paintings by Signac, Van Dongen, Dufy, Bonnard and others in rooms lit by refracted Saint-Tropez sunshine. Outside, the quay space is crowded with contemporary artists, trying their best to sell their colourful works.

The Old Town

A short walk behind the Quai Jean-Jaurès will take you to the **old town** – through an arcade by La Ponche (the old fishing port), past narrow old buildings now housing expensive hotels and boutiques, to the 17th-century **Citadelle** on top of the hill.

The moat, surrounded with greenery, is living quarters for preening peacocks, a few ducks and deer. The Musée de la Marine here contains souvenirs of a local hero, Admiral de Suffren (who took his fleet on an odyssey around the Cape of Good Hope in 1781), model ships and diving equipment.

The Beaches

Saint-Tropez is noted for its beaches. Nearby ones such as the **Plage des Graniers** and the **Bouillabaisse** are popular

*P*astel façades, ship-shape yachts and a colourful crowd: Saint-Tropez has lost none of its legend.

with local people on weekends, but holiday visitors look down their noses at them. They drive out to **Les Salins** or the vast sandy crescent (9.5km or 6 miles long) that stretches in front of green vineyards from **Tahiti Beach** via Pampelonne to Cap Camarat.

Smooth sanded and bordering a clear aquamarine sea, the beaches are fully equipped in summer with all manner of huts and shacks to furnish mattresses, umbrellas and sustenance to sunbathers. (Part of the beach is traditionally given over to nudists.) Every summer the beautiful people gravitate to the bar/restaurant/beach of the moment.

MORE PORTS AND HILL TOWNS

Saint-Tropez is surrounded by delightful spots to visit when you have had enough of the beach scene.

A short trip will take you on to **Gassin** and **Ramatuelle** – towns with panoramic views and pleasant restaurants – and **84** the **Moulins de Paillas**, now fallen in ruins. They provide an introduction to the **Maures** mountains, the oldest geological mass of Provence: worn-down cristalline hills, green and covered with pines and scrub trees.

Going north into the Maures over a long road full of hairpin bends, through thick forests of chestnut and cork, you come to **La Garde-Freinet**. At 405m (1,328ft), the town is considerably cooler than the coast. It has a natural, unspoilt charm that attracts crowd-weary Parisians and Francophile Brits. It also makes a living off the land – cork and chestnuts are major industries.

The ruins of an old fortress evoke the last stand of the marauding Saracens. For several centuries these pirates of Arab origin managed to hold out here as they pillaged the towns below – until they were thrown out in 973.

If you're pressed for time, head stright for **Grimaud** – best in the late afternoon, when you can look out to sea through Provençal lotus trees and enjoy a drink in a café.

Grimaud was the fiefdom of Gibalin (Ghibelline) de Grimaldi. The fortress ruins stand up in piles of stony remnants against a grassy hill. A sign warns of the danger of falling rocks, but you can take a look at the simple, barrel-vaulted 11th-century Templars' church (this is a restored version) and the arcaded charterhouse.

Port-Grimaud, 6.5km or 4 miles downhill on the bay of Saint-Tropez, is the French modern version of Venice. Designed by François Spoerry and opened in 1964, it is a series of artificial canals built on marshland, lined with pleasant houses and flowered terraces painted in the same cool pastel shades as Saint-Tropez.

For most French people, the Côte d'Azur stops at Saint-Tropez (some even say Saint-Raphaël), but the coast does go on. Not always the prettiest stretch, it is spoiled in parts by 20th-century concrete blocks. Still reasonably pleasant, however, are a string of small resort towns – **Cavalaire**, **La Croix-Valmer**, **Pramousquier** and **Rayol** – all in beautiful flowered settings under the Maures hills.

Le Lavandou, originally a colourful spot, has suffered from urbanism, though it's still quite popular. The town has a pretty beachside promenade and is a good starting-point for excursions. From here, go uphill and you'll come to **Bormes-les-Mimosas**, a lovely retreat that lives up to its name – blooming not only with mimosa, but also oleander, roses, geraniums and bougainvillea.

Hyères is the 'granny' of Mediterranean resorts. French holiday-makers were coming to this picturesque old city, attracted by its extremely mild climate, as early as in the 18th century, even before the English started to winter in Nice. Queen Victoria occasionally chose to stay here on her visits to the Côte d'Azur.

On the Place de la République, you'll see a 13th-century **church** where Louis IX, King of France, prayed after his return from a crusade in 1254; Hyères was the landing port for returning crusaders, though they disembarked at **85** what is now the centre of town. Today, modern boulevards run right over the old harbour.

Hyères is a busy city featuring an uphill market street, Rue Massillon (go in the morning when it's in full swing), the old town, an ancient Templars' building and the Eglise Saint-Paul (a Gothic church renovated in the 16th century). From the square there is a splendid panoramic view.

ILES D'HYÈRES

Also known as the Iles d'Or (golden isles) because of their shiny, mica-shot rocks – sometimes mistaken for gold – they are made up of three islands: Levant, Port-Cros and Porquerolles. You can easily visit them by taking a ferry across from Hyères and Le Lavandou or even from the ports of Toulon or Cavalaire.

The long, rocky **Ile du Levant** is France's nudist capital, where one of the first nudist colonies was established in the early 1930s, but you can, of course, also keep your trousers on. The eastern half of the island is seriously off-limits – there is a naval base here.

Next to the Levant lies the **Ile de Port-Cros**, festooned with steep myrtle- and heather-decked hills and an abundance of bird life. This protected national park boasts its own resident flamingos, turtle-doves, cormorants and puffins, as well as rare flowers, orchids, and mushrooms when it's the season (mainly tasty boletus and chanterelles).

The largest island, **Porquerolles**, 7 by 3km (or 4½ by 2 miles) long, is another totally enchanting setting, with lovely sandy beaches along its north shore (where the boat lands), vineyards and pine-woods in the interior, and a southern shoreline of steep, rocky cliffs.

You'll find some excellent small beaches and coves on all three islands – ideal for bathing – but you probably won't be alone in the high season.

Relax under a cool arcade at Port-Grimaud, and watch life go by on the city's canals.

Toulon to Marseilles

TOULON

Pop. 168,000

Military buffs love **Toulon**, France's big naval port, which reeks of maritime history. Its picturesque seafront was devastated during World War II, but even now, with its modern concrete seaport blocks, the town retains a certain dignity.

The city was pushed into prominence in the 17th century by Cardinal Richelieu, who saw the potential of Toulon's great natural harbour. Under Louis XIV, the great military engineer Vauban was commissioned to fortify and enlarge the facilities.

The Second World War was a tragedy for the naval centre. Nearly the whole French fleet was scuttled on 27 November 1942, to keep it from falling into German hands. Two years later the port was battered by Allied troops, and then the Germans blew up their installations before leaving, wreaking

still more havoc. With modern reconstruction, however, Toulon has regained its former importance.

The Old Town and the Port

Broad and busy Boulevard de Strasbourg (off Place de la Liberté) runs through the heart of Toulon, slicing the city in half. To the north is the newer, more residential area; to the south, the remains of the **vieille ville** (old town). Head in this direction for Place Puget, a charming Provençal square set just behind the Municipal Theatre, graced with a dolphin fountain and lots of greenery. Downhill is the narrow market street, Rue d'Alger, a favourite for evening strolling.

Off to the left, the cathedral, **Sainte-Marie-Majeure** (also known as Sainte-Marie-de-la-Seds), has a handsome baroque façade and 18th-century belfry. Another block east is the Cours Lafayette, one of the most animated indoor/outdoor market streets in Europe, where you can buy everything from flowers to leather souvenirs. History enthusiasts can visit the nearby **Musée Historique du Vieux-Toulon**.

The **port** is a particularly lively and interesting part of town. Look out for the magnificently muscled caryatids (by Atlantes de Puget, dating from the 17th century) on the façade of the **Mairie d'Honneur** on the Quai Stalingrad. They represent Strength and Weariness, and do look as if they were shouldering the world – they are about all that's left of the old port. The **Musée Naval** (closed Tuesday in low season) contains some impressive boat models.

The City Centre

Across from the public garden in the west central part of town are the **Musée d'Art** and **Muséum d'Histoire Naturelle** (both closed on bank holidays). The former has a collection of contemporary art and paintings from the Provençal school (17th to 20th century).

Mont Faron, standing at 584m (1,778ft), commands a grandiose view of Toulon, the surrounding hills and mountains and the coast. You can get there by car via a steep, sinuous route or take a *téléphérique* from the Faron Corniche (Gare Inférieure, Boulevard Amiral-Vence). At the top you will find a wooded park, picnic areas, children's play areas, restaurants and a zoo. Close by is the **Tour Beaumont**, a war museum containing information about the Liberation of Provence.

Inland Excursions

Inland excursions from Toulon include **Le Gros Cerveau** ridge for a magnificent panorama, the rugged **Gorges d'Ollioules**, the 16th-century castle remnants of **Evenos** and another look-out point at **Mont Caume** (though access is limited by the military).

If you have time to venture further north, the **Massif de la Sainte-Baume** has the irregular hilly landscape and *maquis* typical of Provence, a venerable forest and a stunning view from **Saint-Pilon**. **89**

Côte des Calanques

The limestone coastline between Toulon and Marseilles is riddled with deep, uneven inlets (*calanques*). This stretch, backed by the green scrub of the *maquis*, has spawned a variety of holiday developments, but you can still find attractive natural sites.

Well-sheltered **Sanary**, with sandy beaches and an old port, is the first town you come to on the Baies du Soleil (Sunny Bays). **Bandol** takes the honours as the area's leading resort. It has a mild climate and long beach lined with housing developments, and is known for its vineyards which produce good red and white wine.

You can make a pleasant side trip to the privately owned island of **Bendor**. This site boasts a reproduction of a Provençal village and museums devoted to the sea and to wine.

One of the world's largest shipyards up until a few years ago, **La Ciotat** has managed to retain a small bit of its original charm. Now that the background of towering cranes and steel hulls of the once busy shipyard have gone, there only remains the old fishing port – a typically Provençal backdrop of nets, small, bright boats and colourful houses. Tourism is now being developed.

Dip your toe or have a swim – the water on the Côte des Calanques always looks inviting!

The port of **Cassis** may well seem familiar – paintings of the harbour by artists like Matisse, Vlaminck and Dufy hang in museums all over the world. What you'll see today are the same gaily-coloured stucco houses and crisp little triangular sails bobbing on the clear blue water. Hovering in the background are the rocks of La Gardiole and the tree-covered Cap Canaille, at 427m (some 1,400ft) the highest cliff in all of Continental Europe.

Cassis is mainly known for its incomparable shellfish, its *bouillabaisse* (fish soup) and its white wine, appreciated all over the south – not to be confused with *cassis*, the blackcurrant syrup or liqueur.

From Cassis you'll probably want to visit some *calanques*, best done in a rented boat or on a tour (several companies operate from the port). The most spectacular of them all is the **calanque d'En Vau** – a mini-fjord with limpid blue-green water fingering through the rocky cliffs to a minute crescent of a white beach – perfect for a spot of bathing.

Marseilles

Though not really part of the Côte d'Azur, this great city (*Marseille* to the French) merits a visit for many reasons. France's largest port, its second largest metropolis and its oldest, Marseilles has played a major role in the country's history. The *Berlitz Pocket Guide to Provence* has more detailed information on this bustling, fascinating place.

Marseilles offers excellent shopping (try the streets off the famous **Canebière** thoroughfare), a colourful, international atmosphere, big industry, interesting museums and very good food: some of the best *bouillabaisse* on the coast is to be found here, particularly around the **vieux port** (old port) and on the Corniche (Vallon des Auffres).

Be sure to wander around the old port, first used by the Phocaeans in 600BC, now full of yachts and motor launches. You shouldn't miss the impressive facilities of the modern port either. (You can also tour it by boat.)

91

What to Do

Shopping

Where to Shop

Shopping is a delight on the Côte d'Azur, with an enormous choice of both merchandise and types of shops in which to indulge at leisure.

For the best possible selection at unbeatable prices, go to one of the **hypermarchés** (hypermarkets) that are situated on the outskirts of all major towns. As well as an incomparable food section, you will also find clothes, sports goods, books, and household and gardening equipment. In addition there are frequently dozens (sometimes hundreds) of independent smaller shops and restaurants under the same roof. Major credit cards are usually accepted, extensive free parking is provided and normal opening hours are from Monday to Saturday from 9am to 9pm (often later in summer).

Non-stop opening hours, however, are not the norm in other shops. A long leisurely lunch break is still almost sacrosanct throughout the Midi: southern French opening hours are from 8 or 9am to noon and 3 or 4pm to 7 or 8pm.

On a smaller scale than the giant hypermarkets, **department stores** like the Galeries Lafayette are located on the main shopping street of cities such as Nice, Toulon and Marseilles. They tend to specialize in clothing, including a variety of designer labels, but also sell well-known perfumery and cosmetic brands, food, household equipment and interesting gifts/souvenirs at reasonable prices. They offer a duty-free service to non-EU visitors and accept major credit cards.

City-centre **shopping malls** contain chain stores, and a vast range of high fashion shops to suit every budget.

Chic **boutiques** selling ultra-smart clothes and accessories at ultra-expensive prices abound in all the fashionable coastal resorts and large towns (try the Casino area of Monte Carlo, Rue de France in Nice,

Rue d'Antibes in Cannes, anywhere in Saint-Tropez). Such establishments invariably accept credit cards.

All along the coast you will find plenty of fascinating **craft** workshops displaying a tempting array of top quality original gifts with affordable price tags (for the most part).

Food is a passion with the French, so there is no shortage of specialist shops in every village and town. Often shopping for the delectable delicacies on display is just as much fun as eating them! For convenience food shopping, small super-

Markets are a feature of the Côte d'Azur. Stroll along and pick up a rare find at Cannes.

markets are found everywhere except in the smallest villages. Food shops are usually open Sunday morning, many closing on Monday. (City-centre stores may follow supermarket hours.) *Pâtisseries* sometimes remain open on Sunday afternoon and many bakers have their first batch of bread ready as early as 6am.

93

Markets

The mild climate of the Côte d'Azur makes open-air market-shopping a pleasure, and few visitors can resist the profusion of colourful merchandise on display – fresh fruit and vegetables in abundance, delicate farm-made cheeses, exotic Mediterranean fish, aromatic herbs, traditional Provençal fabrics and local arts and crafts. Market people set up their stalls early: vans and lorries begin to arrive from 5am onwards, so parking may be at a premium. Some larger markets last all day, but most are over by 12.30pm. Here are a few favourites:

Antibes (old town). Regional products: every morning except Monday; craft market: Tuesday, Friday and Sunday morning.

Cannes. General: every morning except Monday; antiques: Saturday.

Fréjus. General: Wednesday and Saturday morning.

Fréjus Plage. General: Tuesday and Friday in summer; crafts: evenings in summer.

Grasse. Regional products: on Saturday and Sunday morning.

Hyères. General: on Tuesday, Wednesday, Thursday and Friday morning.

Menton. Covered market: every morning; antiques: Friday.

Nice (Cour Saleya). Flower market: daily except Monday; regional products: every morning except Monday; antiques: Monday.

Nice (Place Saint-François). Fish: every morning except on Monday.

Saint-Tropez. General: Tuesday and Saturday morning.
Sainte-Maxime. Crafts every evening in summer.
Vence. Regional products: on Tuesday and Friday morning; antiques: Wednesday.

What to Buy

Products from the olive tree: introduced to southern France by the Greeks almost 3,000 years ago, olive trees, with their distinctive knarled trunks and silver-green leaves, are a feature of the regional landscape and their cultivation is an essential element in local culture. Buy olives loose from great tubs in any market or pre-packed in either bottles or plastic containers. The favourite variety on the Côte d'Azur is undoubtedly the small black *olive de Nice*, but look as well for *pitchouline* (a green olive from the Var) and *tanche* (a purple olive from Nyons). Olives may be simply preserved in brine but also come in oil seasoned with herbs, spices and hot peppers. Local olive oil is good value, and a wide

*P*rovençal designs make colourful souvenirs. Crafts are part of a rich, southern tradition.

choice of attractive articles are carved from the olive wood.

A mecca for all things pertaining to the olive tree is Alizari's in the old town of Nice (next to the Opera House), a wonderful shop where olives are stored in barrels and oil is poured from enormous vats.

Herbs grow wild on hillsides all along the coast and inland, but they are also extensively farmed either for selling fresh **95**

or dried. Look for Herbes de Provence – a dried herb mixture often sold in pretty presentation packs; and also dried *bouquets garnis* consisting of a bay leaf and thyme sprig. Alternatively, pick sprigs of sage, rosemary and thyme in the hills and dry them at home.

*R*enoir's house, at Cagnes-sur-Mer, provides the inspiration for latter-day artists.

Fresh fruit and vegetables: buy either from markets, or in season look for roadside stalls selling peaches, strawberries, melons, cherries, etc.

Honey: perfumed with lavender and herbs, it is usually of excellent quality. Buy it from market stalls, or from farms or producers who advertise at the roadside.

Confectionery: local specialities include crystallized fruits and, from Tourettes-sur-Loup (just outside Vence), crystallized violets.

Arts and Crafts: many talented artists and craftspeople work on the coast drawn – as they have been for centuries – by the colourful landscape and wonderful light. *Foires artisanales* (craft fairs) are held throughout the summer, and in coastal resorts, craft stalls are set up every evening during the summer. You will find painters, jewellers, potters, glassblowers, silk-screen painters, wood-carvers, weavers, etc, all selling their wares. The quality varies but overall is extremely professional.

Vallauris has been a pottery town since Roman times and today there are still over 200 potters working there, with at least a dozen showrooms lining the main street. Next door, the pretty village of Biot specializes in glass. Mougins, Vence and Saint-Paul-de-Vence are well known for their art galleries; Tourettes-sur-Loup has a craft quarter in the old town; and the pedestrian streets of Menton are packed with craft and souvenir shops.

Fabrics: traditional Provençal cotton fabrics have gained considerable international popularity in recent years, and are widely available on the coast. Market stalls carry stocks at very reasonable prices. Alternatively, two up-market brands – O Soleïado and Les Olivades – are much more expensive and sell from their own boutiques in all major towns.

Perfumery: Grasse, the 'perfume capital' is the obvious place to go, but small shops also sell locally distilled lavender water, lavender bags, perfumed bath oils and soaps (soap-making is a traditional business of Marseilles).

Santons: look out for these delightful figures dressed in typical Provençal dress. They are on sale throughout the year but are especially associated with Christmas – there are special *santon* fairs during December.

Wine: Provençal wines – red, rosé and white – are excellent value. Among highly regarded Côte d'Azur specialities are wines from Bellet – a small and newly fashionable vineyard in the hills behind Nice; Saint-Tropez with especially good rosés; Bandol and Cassis. Buy the wines in a specialist shop or follow one of the clearly sign-posted *Routes du Vin* (wine roads). For a selection of everyday wines at unbelievably low prices, stop at one of the *caves coopératives* (wine co-operatives) inland in the Var *département*, where wine is sold in bottles or *en vrac* (straight from the barrel). **97**

Sports and Games

Enjoy the outdoor life under the Mediterranean sun: facilities are generally first-rate.

Swimming: the Côte d'Azur has a very good record as regards the cleanliness of its beaches. You will find many excellent sand beaches, as well as those with imported sand, rocks or pebbles. For more details, see p.119.

Water-skiing: *le ski nautique* can be found at all the larger beaches (Cannes, Nice, Antibes and so on). Real daredevils go for kite-skiing.

Windsurfing: *la planche à voile* is a well-established sport along the coast, where boards may be hired. (Courses are run by accredited schools in most resorts.) Experienced surfers especially enjoy the effects of the mistral (the strong westerly wind of Provence) and head straight for Saint-Laurent-du-Var (next to Nice Airport) and the Var coast, particularly the islands off Hyères (see p.86).

Scuba Diving, Snorkelling: The Mediterranean sea-bed offers tremendous scope for divers, but a minimum level of expertise is required. Instruction is available at centres in Nice, Monaco, Cannes, Saint-Raphaël, Antibes, Bandol and

T reading on water or feet firmly in the sand, it's easy to enjoy all the activities which the coast has to offer.

the Ile du Levant (the most easterly of the group of islands off Hyères). Exploration of the *calanques* (see p.90) is based around Bandol; the sea around Hyères Islands contains over 500 shipwrecks dating back centuries – diving from specially equipped boats is possible off the coast at Cavalaire and Le Lavandou.

For further details on these underwater activities, contact the Fédération française de Sports sous-marins, 24, quai Rive Neuve, 13007 Marseille; tel. 91.33.99.31.

Fishing: the fish population of the Mediterranean is suffering from over-fishing and pollution. But you can spend a few pleasant hours with baited hook around the coast, or take

Fishing tall-tales are a local speciality. Back at the harbour, café talk is full of stories about the fish that didn't get away.

a day-tour on a fishing boat. Real sportsmen like to angle for trout in the mountain streams inland. Inquire about licence regulations at the local *Syndicat d'initiative* (tourist office, see p.136) or *Hôtel de Ville* or *Mairie* (town hall).

Boating and Sailing: the coast is lined with first-class yacht facilities. Should you require the finest sea-faring vessel but haven't brought your own boat, why not hire a 30m (98ft) yacht complete with a ten-man crew and enjoy 'the life of Riley'? If more modest requirements will suffice – and for those on a tighter budget – smaller boats are also available all along the coast.

For an idea of what it might cost to hire a boat, see p.132. Cannes and Antibes are the biggest rental centres.

Tennis: tennis courts are plentiful almost everywhere along the coast. The proper attire and payment of an hourly court fee will admit you to most clubs. In summer you may have to book a day ahead.

Golf: Côte d'Azur *parcours de golf* rank among the best in France – with scenic 18-hole courses at Mougins, Valbonne, Biot, Mandelieu-La-Napoule (all clustered around Cannes), Monte Carlo (Mont-Agel), as well as a few 9-hole courses.

You can hire clubs on the spot, though it's advisable to bring your own shoes and golf balls, as these are expensive in France.

Horse-riding: there are lots of possibilities for riding, often 'ranch' style in the countryside behind the coast.

Skiing: about two hours from the coast are 11 winter sports areas, some very well developed. The best-known are Isola 2000 (where they teach the new graduated short-ski method), Auron and Valberg.

Other Activities: you can play the local *pétanque* (also called *boules*) if the natives will initiate you to this bowling game. Every type of sport, however, is available in the main resorts – from regular bowling, judo and archery to table tennis (contact the local tourist office). If you're feeling fit, hire a bicycle and pedal around the hills alongside the dedicated amateurs. The region's modern racecourse is at Cros-de-Cagnes, near Nice airport.

Entertainment

The Côte d'Azur offers a stupendous choice of distractions to appeal to every possible taste. Both Nice and Monte Carlo have an **opera house** staging a comprehensive programme of concerts, ballet and opera year-round, but during the summer months there are jazz festivals and classical concerts throughout the region. Even the smallest village has a patron saint's day with processions, children's games and usually a dance in the evening. Some are quite grand affairs, lasting a week or more, with marquees and large orchestras; others may just be a disco in the village square.

Any excuse is good for a get-together, and there are hundreds of **festivals** celebrating anything from the first day of spring to the end of harvest. However, major events such as the Mardi Gras carnivals in February, attract visitors from all over the world.

As for **nightlife**, sophisticated floorshows and elegant dinner-dancing venues are to **101**

CALENDAR OF EVENTS

January *Monte Carlo*: Automobile rally. *Cannes*: MIDEM: international recording and music-publishing fair.

February *Nice* (two weeks preceeding Shrove Tuesday): Mardi Gras carnival. *Menton* (second two weeks): citrus festival. *Monaco* (first week): circus festival.

April *Monte Carlo*: tennis championships.

May *Cannes*: international film festival. *Monte Carlo*: Monaco Grand Prix. *Grasse* (mid-month): Rose festival. *Saint-Tropez* (8th, 17-19th): Bravades – costumed processions celebrating the town's patron saint.

June *Saint-Tropez* (15th). Bravade des Espagnols, celebrating victory over the Spanish fleet in 1637.

July Bastille Day (14th) with dancing and fireworks in every town and village. *Antibes/Juan-les-Pins*: jazz festival. *Nice/Cimiez*: jazz festival. *Ramatuelle*: jazz festival. *Le Lavandou*: international folklore festival. *Les Issambres*: craft fair.

August *Fréjus* (throughout the month): Grande Féria (bullfighting). *Roquebrune-Cap-Martin* (mid-month): antiques fair. *Ramatuelle* (mid-month): theatre festival. *Monaco*: firework festival on five evenings. *Grasse*: Fête du jasmin with decorated floats, parades and folk dancing. *Menton* (throughout the month): open-air classical music festival.

September *Roquebrune-Cap-Martin* (mid-month): antiques fair. *Cagnes-sur-Mer* (1st two weeks): antiques fair. *Puget-Theniers* (first two weeks): Patron Saint's Festival.

October *Cannes*: international puppet festival. VIDCOM: International video fair.

November *Le Lavandou* (early): flea market.

December *Cannes*: international festival of dance. *Bandol* (5th): wine fair.

be found at international hotels in Nice, Cannes and Monte Carlo. Discothèques flourish at all the coastal resorts, but those of Saint-Tropez, Monte Carlo, Nice and Cannes probably attract the most fashionable clientele.

Gambling has been an indispensable element of Côte d'Azur attractions ever since the 19th century. The Monte Carlo Casino has the most cachet, and is the most lavish and well-known, but many resorts between Sainte-Maxime and Menton have their own

Nothing spells glamour more than the Côte d'Azur – except the Cannes Film Festival.

casino. The smarter ones will require guests to be conservatively dressed; some charge an entrance fee (Monte Carlo is free); and although operating hours vary greatly, general opening times are from 3pm until early morning. (Remember you may be asked to show your passport.)

103

There are facilities for every type of gambling – non-stop slot-machines, blackjack and poker, and the French games of chance such as roulette and baccara.

Children

Children are extremely well catered for on the Côte d'Azur and are unlikely to be bored. Apart from some excellent beaches (remember to bring suntan lotion to protect young skins from the scorching mid-day sun) with all the usual watersport facilities, inland the moutain resorts of Valberg, Isola and Auron offer a wide range of summer activities as well as skiing in winter.

There are **zoos** at Sanary-sur-Mer, Toulon and Cap Ferrat (with a chimpanzee show every afternoon) plus a safari park at Fréjus (open daily 10am to 5pm, entrance fee 55F for adults, 33F for children).

Marineland at Antibes is a winner with kids – a marine zoo with penguins, seals and an afternoon dolphin show –

but is expensive at 93F for adults, 62F for children (open daily 10am to 7pm). On the same site **Aquasplash**, a water games park, is open from June to September only, entrance fee 70F. Crazy golf is also available here and at Le Grand Jardin – a children's play park at Le Lavandou.

OK Corral is a Wild West theme park on the RN8 north of Bandol (open March-Nov, 10am to 6.30pm, entrance fee 60F) and youngsters will adore **La Petite Ferme Provençale** at Antibes, where there are baby farm animals to bottle-feed, goats to milk and pony rides. Open daily 10am to 6pm, entrance fee 36F.

The **Musée Océanographique** at Monaco (see p.42) has an exceptional aquarium, while the **Musée National** features a superb collection of dolls and automated toys. (Open daily except during the Monaco Grand Prix in May from 10am to 6.30pm; entrance fee 26F for adults and 15F for children.) Monaco's **Jardin Exotique**, with its extensive collection of bizzare cacti, is also popular.

Eating Out

Wining and dining on the Côte d'Azur is pure, unadulterated pleasure, whether it is a simple snack at a pavement café, a romantic dinner served under the stars, or one of the superb gastronomic meals created by a master-chef in an internationally acclaimed restaurant.

Whatever your taste, you can be sure to find it here, in this sunny corner of France, where food seems to take on an altogether special definition and individuality.

The essence of southern French food is its emphasis on colour and full flavour, with fresh, basic ingredients such as tomatoes, garlic, onions, fresh herbs and olive oil. Naturally, fish is an important ingredient in coastal areas and, of course, bread accompanies everything. In the extreme east, the Italian influence is strong, with a variety of pasta dishes appearing on menus. Salads are firm favourites during the hot summer months and fresh fruit – strawberries, raspberries, cherries, peaches, nectarines and melons – are plentiful.

WHEN TO EAT

The Côte d'Azur is notably cosmopolitan, but traditional French eating habits are fairly rigid. **Breakfast** is a meagre affair of coffee and croissants,

*F*or an unforgettable gastronomic experience, look no further than the world-renowned 'Moulin'.

although some hotels now offer a more substantial buffet. For many people, especially in rural areas, **lunch** is served promptly at noon, and supper, taken around 8 or 8.30pm, usually consists of nothing more than a bowl of soup and a salad or omelette.

Holiday-makers, however, will probably prefer to have a snack or picnic lunch (you will find plenty of pre-cooked takeaway goodies for a picnic from any good butcher or *traiteur*) with a proper **dinner** at night. In the really smart resorts, restaurant service in the evening may continue until 10 or even 11pm, but do not depend upon it in smaller towns where last orders could be no later than 9pm, sometimes even earlier. In addition to *à la carte* dishes off the main menu, most restaurants offer a choice of one or two set menus. These offer good value for money and may even have wine included.

WHAT TO EAT

Soup and Salad

Pistou is a substantial summertime vegetable and pasta soup taking its name from the *pistou* (a garlic and fresh basil

*T*antalizing tarts, fresh fruit and vegetables – the art of good living has never been so simple.

paste to which Parmesan may be added around Nice) which is stirred in at the last minute. Additional grated cheese can be added to individual taste. On a hot mid-summer evening, it can be a meal in itself served with crusty bread, some fruit and a glass of chilled wine.

Soupe de poisson is made from small fish left over from the main catch, which are simmered with tomatoes and saffron, then puréed and sieved. It is always served with toasted bread which should be rubbed with garlic cloves, spread with *rouille* (a pink, garlicky mayonnaise) and topped with grated cheese.

In a **bourrade**, the fish is left in chunks and the sauce thickened with mayonnaise.

Speaking of garlic, try a bracing **aïoli** – when you don't have any important social engagements – dipping boiled fish, potatoes, green beans and so on in the heavily perfumed mayonnaise.

The popular **salade niçoise** is a much-maligned dish. At its simple best, it consists of tomatoes, anchovies and black olives moistened with olive oil and vinegar. Optional extras include raw vegetables such as sweet peppers, radishes, cucumber, young broad beans or artichokes, onions, tuna fish and hard-boiled eggs. Lettuce and any cooked vegetables are anathema to purists.

Endless mixed salads are offered, many with seafood or ham and cheese. **Salade antiboise** usually combines cooked diced fish and anchovy fillets with green peppers, beetroot, rice and capers with vinaigrette dressing. **Crudités**, a raw vegetable salad, makes a nice, light first course.

Fish

Sardines are the most common locally caught fish, which may be served very plainly dipped in hot oil and fried until crispy. To eat, hold by the tail **107**

and bite off a filet either side without bones. They can also be filleted, opened flat, dipped in batter, fried in hot oil and served with a wedge of lemon (*beignets de sardine*). Another local speciality is to sandwich two fillets together with a filling of finely chopped Swiss chard leaves, then fry or grill the fish (*sardines farcies*). Simplest of all is to marinate raw fillets in lemon juice until they turn opaque and are 'cooked' (*sardines marinées*).

The aristocrat of fish is the **loup de mer** (sea bass), best prepared with fennel, flamed. **Daurade**, a tender white fish (sea bream), costs less. It is usually grilled or baked with onion, tomato, lemon juice and a dash of wine, occasionally with garlic and a *pastis* (aniseed) flavouring. **Rouget** (red mullet) may be served grilled or *en papillote* (baked in foil with lemon wedges).

The **scampi** (prawns) that appear on menus everywhere can be good, but they're invariably imported and frozen. **Langouste**, or spiny lobster, costs a king's ransom. It's

eaten with mayonnaise or hot in a tomato-and-cognac-flavoured sauce (*à l'américaine*).

Mussels (*moules*) are popular in white wine (*à la marinière*), in soup or with savoury stuffings. A lowly but tempting gourmandise is **friture de mer**, fried small fish which are eaten like French fries.

Meat and Poultry

Steak turns up in various guises; the good cuts (*entrecôte, côte de bœuf, faux-filet, filet*) are as tasty charcoal-grilled as with sauces. *Bleu* means almost raw; *saignant*, rare; and *à point*, medium.

In springtime, **lamb** is particularly succulent; you'll often see *gigot d'agneau* or *côtes d'agneau grillées aux herbes* (leg of lamb or grilled chops with herbs), which the French serve medium rare. *Brochettes*, or skewered kebabs, can be delicious, though the quality depends on the meat.

Daube de bœuf, a traditional beef stew, is particularly good in Nice. With its aromatic brown, wine-flavoured mushroom sauce, accompanied by freshly made noodles (*pâtes fraîches*), it can be truly memorable. **Estouffade**, a variation on the theme, adds black olives to the sauce.

Veal dishes are often of Italian inspiration, as in breaded escalopes milanaises (*scaloppini*). But *alouettes sans têtes* are not 'headless larks' as the translation would imply: they are small rolled veal cutlets with stuffing (veal birds).

Even tripe-haters are converted by the Niçois version of this dish (**tripes niçoises**): a superb concoction simmered in olive oil, white wine, tomato, onion, garlic and herbs. **Pieds et paquets**, a Marseilles speciality, consists of stuffed tripe and sheeps' trotters simmered with bacon, onion, carrots, white wine, garlic and sometimes tomato.

Chicken is frequently spit-roasted with herbs (*poulet rôti aux herbes*); *poulet niçois* is a fricassée made with white wine, stock, herbs, tomatoes and black olives. **Rabbit** (*lapin*) can be quite tender, and might be served in a mustard sauce or *à la provençale*.

In season (autumn/winter), the menu may list **partridge** (*perdreau*), **pigeon** or **quail** (*caille*) often served with a grape sauce (*aux raisins*), or **boar** (*marcassin* or *sanglier*).

Oysters galore! Fresh seafood is still a delight on the Côte d'Azur despite the high price tags.

Pasta and Vegetables

The Italian influence is strong around Menton and Nice, becoming less so as you travel further west, and pasta here rivals any in Italy – but with subtle differences.

Ravioli and **cannelloni** are served with tomato sauce or meat gravy, both topped with grated cheese, either Parmesan or gruyère *rapé* (grated gruyère or emmental). **Lasagne** is popular and **fettucini**, **tagliatelle** or **spaghetti** are frequently served as an accompaniment to a main meat dish, a practice rarely seen in Italy. **Gnocchis** (small, feather-light balls of semolina and/or mashed potato) are sprinkled with grated gruyère cheese and accompany meat dishes.

But the glory of southern France is its fresh vegetables. **Ratatouille** – the celebrated vegetable stew, a delicious concoction of tomatoes, aubergine (eggplant), onions, courgette (zucchini) and green peppers – practically stands as a meal in itself, either hot or cold. You'll also find tomatoes stuffed with bread crumbs, garlic and parsley (**tomates à la Provençale**) and a variety of baked summer vegetables – aubergines, courgettes, peppers, even onions and potatoes – stuffed with their own chopped flesh, breadcrumbs or rice, garlic, herbs, minced meat and grated cheese (*les farcis*).

*T*he flavours of the south: fresh herbs, sun-ripened olives, tangy lemons and a glass of rosé wine.

The great stuffed vegetable speciality of the region, however, is **chou fassum** (stuffed cabbage) from Grasse. Local housewives detach and blanch the outer leaves, then blanch and roughly chop the inner leaves which are mixed with rice, eggs, cheese, herbs and minced meat. The cabbage is reassembled with the stuffing contained within the outer leaves and tied up in a large net bag (a *fassum*) and simmered for a couple of hours.

Asparagus (*asperges*) are superb served warm with melted butter or hollandaise sauce or cold with vinaigrette. **Artichokes** receive the same treatment or may appear with meat or herb stuffings.

Cheese and Dessert

In the south you can usually eat the well-known classics from the 300-odd varieties of French **cheese**. Don't miss out on the regionally made goat- or sheeps' milk cheeses, however (*fromages de chèvre, de brebis*). A few good names to remember and try: *tomme de Sospel, tomme de chèvre de montagne, brousse de la Vésubie, cabécou, poivre d'âne*.

For dessert, nothing can rival the local **fruits** in season. Savour the fat, dark-red strawberries (April-October) dipped in *crème fraîche* (a slightly sharp double cream). Melons of all kinds (from Cavaillon, near Aix, they're renowned) taste sweeter than usual. Figs and peaches are equally good. **Ice-creams** are refreshing, especially the fruit **sorbets**. You can satisfy a sweet tooth with all kinds of fruit tarts and local **pastries**: *ganses* (small fried cakes topped with sugar), *pignons* (buttery croissants with pine-nuts) and the famed *tarte tropézienne* of Saint-Tropez – a rich, delicious yellow cake with custard filling and coarse-sugar topping.

Quick Snacks

Cafés serve hearty **sandwiches** on long chunks of French bread, pâté, ham or cheese being the most common fillings. Thin-sliced bread (*pain de mie*) is used for the delicious **111** *croque-monsieur* (toasted ham and cheese sandwich). **Omelettes** are always reliable fare.

A local speciality, **tian** takes its name from the local, oval-shaped earthenware gratin dish (good gifts to take home for enthusiastic cooks), but also applies to any food cooked in a *tian*. Most popular is *tian de courgettes* – a savoury egg, rice and courgette custard flavoured with garlic and herbs; and *tian de sardines*.

Traditionally summer picnic fare, the *tarte aux blettes* is a thick, tasty omelette green-flecked with finely chopped Swiss chard leaves and usually served cold. Be sure to sample **socca** – a great speciality in the old town of Nice. An enormous wood-oven baked pancake made from chick pea flour, it must be eaten piping hot straight from the pan.

Another popular local item (perfect for the beach) is **pan bagnat** – essentially a huge round sandwich filled with tomatoes, hard-boiled egg, anchovies, olives, and sliced raw onions, moistened with a dash of olive oil.

Also noteworthy are the excellent thin-crusted **pizzas** in a variety of flavours but always served with a bottle of fiery-flavoured olive oil spiced with hot peppers and herbs for sprinkling over. **Pissaladière** is an open onion tart, flavoured with anchovies and topped with black olives.

Aperitifs and Wine

Local Provençal **wines** tend to be relatively light and are perfectly suited to both the climate and the cuisine. Rosés, always served well-chilled, are very much a speciality, and appreciated by locals and visitors alike. They are served before a meal as an apéritif, but can also be sipped at any time of day. The whites are particularly good with seafood and the reds (sometimes served very lightly chilled in summer) can stand up to any meat.

The best regional wines bear an *appellation d'origine contrôlée* (A.O.C.) label, guaranteeing both place of origin and government-controlled quality. Four areas are given these labels: La Palette, Cassis, Bandol and Bellet.

La Palette (grown at Meyreuil, near Aix-en-Provence) comes from country thick with pines and herbs, whose fresh fragrances are said to permeate the wines. They exist in red and white, the most notable being Château Simone. **Cassis** produces a fine red wine, but the flowery, light white wine is a special treat, particularly with shellfish.

Near Toulon, **Bandol** wine grows in a particularly favoured setting, producing some whites and lots of fruity rosés and reds – the latter are particularly good; look for Domaine des Tempiers.

Bellet is the fourth A.O.C. area, on precariously-sloped vineyards above Nice, producing white, red and rosé wines.

Tavel and Lirac, two **rosés** grown near Avignon, are famous. The colour of rosé is important: it should be light to rosy pink, not orange, which indicates that the wine has oxidized prematurely.

The favourite **apéritif** on the coast is undoubtedly *pastis*

Rosé wine is the perfect companion to Mediterranean dishes. Why not take some home?

– a golden aniseed-flavoured liquid which turns milky when water is added. With a dash of red grenadine liqueur, it becomes a *tomate*. Alternatively, try a *kir* (white wine with a dash of blackcurrant liqueur). Yet another delicious possibility is rosé wine with a dash of peach syrup. *Santé!*

To Help You Order ...

Do you have a table for ...?	**Avez-vous une table pour ...?**		
Do you have a set-price menu?	**Avez-vous un menu à prix fixe?**		

I'd like a/an/some ...	**J'aimerais ...**		
beer	**une bière**	menu	**la carte**
butter	**du beurre**	milk	**du lait**
bread	**du pain**	mineral water	**de l'eau minérale**
coffee	**un café**		
dessert	**un dessert**	potatoes	**des pommes de terre**
fish	**du poisson**		
French fries	**des frites**	salad	**une salade**
fruit	**un fruit**	soup	**du potage**
glass	**un verre**	sugar	**du sucre**
ice-cream	**une glace**	tea	**du thé**
meat	**de la viande**	wine	**du vin**

... and Read the Menu

agneau	lamb	**crevettes**	shrimps
ail	garlic	**écrevisse**	crayfish
anchois	anchovy	**endive**	chicory/endive
asperges	asparagus		
aubergine	aubergine/eggplant	**épinards**	spinach
		fèves	broad beans
bifteck	steak	**flageolets**	kidney beans
bœuf	beef	**foie**	liver
canard	duck	**fraises**	strawberries
cervelle	brains	**fruits de mer**	seafood
chou	cabbage	**haricots verts**	string beans
côte, côtelette	chop, cutlet	**jambon**	ham
courgettes	courgette/zucchini	**langoustine**	prawn
		lapin	rabbit

BLUEPRINT
for a
Perfect Trip

An A–Z Summary of Practical Information

> Listed after many entries is the appropriate French translation, usually in the singular, as well as a number of phrases that may come in handy during your stay in France.

A

ACCOMMODATION (See also CAMPING on p.120, YOUTH HOSTELS on p.139 and the list of RECOMMENDED HOTELS starting on p.66)

Despite its reputation as one of the world's glamour spots, not all accommodation on the Côte d'Azur falls into the ultra-expensive category. While the area has more than its fair share of internationally known luxury hotels, it is possible to find a wide range of very acceptable accommodation to fit all budgets. Official classification is from one to four stars (some hotels are outside this classification but this does not imply that they are inferior) and the overall quality is good. However, the best establishments within each price range are extremely popular and advance booking is advised.

Apart from hotels in the one-star range, most rooms have a private bath or shower/WC, telephone and TV. Three-star rooms will also have additional facilities such as hairdryer, minibar, etc, and may have air-conditioning. Swimming pools are commonly found (except in some town-centre hotels) but not all hotels have a restaurant although breakfast is usually provided – at an extra charge. Only luxury hotels have room service and an in-house laundry. Ironing facilities and tea/coffee-making equipment are practically unknown in French hotels. Reception staff frequently speak English.

Peak season. July and August are peak months when prices are highest and rooms at a premium. During May – when both the Cannes Film Festival and Monaco Grand Prix are staged – every room from Saint-Tropez to the Italian border is booked months, sometimes years, in advance. If you intend to be here at that time, plan well ahead.

Low season. The larger centres such as Nice, Cannes and Monte Carlo arrange spectacular low season events and have a calendar of international conferences to attract visitors throughout the winter. Many hotels, however, particularly inland and in smaller seaside resorts, close during these months. Those that do remain open frequently offer substantial reductions in room rates, representing excellent value for money.

If booking ahead, a **deposit** or *arrhes* will be required. For last-minute bookings without a deposit, the reservation will usually be honoured until 6pm, but may be given to another client if you have not arrived or telephoned to explain before that time.

TYPES OF HOTEL

Relais et Châteaux. These hotels, covering the whole of France, offer several tempting possibilities. All are four-star establishments, some in historical buildings. Their brochure is available from the tourist office (see p.136).

Relais du Silence. A chain of two- to four-star hotels in particularly scenic settings. Some are genuine old stagecoach inns. Establishments are listed in a free booklet published annually and available from the tourist office (see p.136).

Logis de France. Small or medium-sized, family-run restaurant/hotels, mostly in the one- or two-star bracket, almost all of which lie in the villages or countryside outside urban areas. The *Logis de France* publish an annual guide (free if requested from the French national tourist offices abroad). Although each establishment can be very different, their charter requires a personalized welcome, regional cooking using local produce and clear-cut, all-inclusive prices. Because **117**

they are usually relatively small and very popular, they fill up quickly. Book ahead or get in early.

Hôtellerie Familiale. Very similar in intention to the *Logis*, they issue a free annual booklet detailing the amenities of each establishment in their area. The headquarters for the region are: Fédération française des logis et auberges de France, Chambre régionale de commerce et d'industrie (CRCI), 8, rue Neuve-Saint-Martin, BP 1880, 13222 Marseille; tel. 91.91.92.48.

Table d'Hôte/Chambre d'Hôte. These are private individuals, generally in rural areas, offering meals and/or rooms. For a taste of 'real' France, they are well worth a try. They are signposted at convenient points, or posted on boards outside the house or farm. A *chambre d'hôte* room will include the cost of breakfast.

Gîtes Ruraux. The *Gîtes Ruraux* is an official body with regional offices, which oversees the organization of self-catering holiday accommodation (all-year round) and sets the standards. Accommodation is usually in charming old regional houses or renovated farm buildings. Certain minimal standards of comfort (running water, toilets, kitchen facilities, etc) are required. Each *gîte* houses a fixed number of guests, and is rented by the week. You can book either by writing or telephoning the addresses below (*Service des Réservations, Gîtes de France*), or by writing to the owners listed on the white pages of the catalogue, with all conditions obtainable from the same address.

Alpes Maritimes: CRT 55, BP 602 06011 Nice Cedex 1; tel. 93.44.39.39.

Var: Conseil Général, Rond-Point du 4/12/74, BP 215, 83006 Draguinan Cedex; tel. 94.67.10.40.

Do you have a single/double room for tonight?	**Avez-vous une chambre pour une/deux personne(s) pour cette nuit?**
with bath/shower/toilet	**avec bain/douche/toilette**
What's the rate per night?	**Quel est le prix pour une nuit?**

AIRPORTS (aéroport)

Nice-Côte d'Azur is the main international airport (tel. 93.21.30.30) with scheduled connections from all major European cities, North Africa and some American cities. **Héliair Monaco** operates a regular helicopter service between the airport and Monaco which takes 7 minutes; price 360F; tel. 92.05.00.50. Seating is limited, so it is advisable to book in advance through your travel agent.

Buses depart from the airport for all main destinations along the coast and a shuttle takes passengers into Nice, stopping at major hotels and the mainline station. Some hotels run their own free minibus service. Taxis are also readily available.

In addition **Marseille-Marignane** (tel. 91.39.36.36), with international scheduled connections, serves the western Côte d'Azur. There are bus connections to coastal resorts and a service to Nice Airport via the *autoroute* (motorway) A8.

B

BEACHES (la plage)

The Côte d'Azur is proud of its record for clean beaches. Sea-water analysis is carried out regularly and some beaches are swept early every morning in season. Although there are many superb expanses of natural sand, some beaches (notably at Monaco, Nice and Cannes) are created with imported sand.

Most beaches are free and can be very crowded in July and August. Private beaches attached to luxury hotels may be for residents only, though some may admit non-residents for a fee. Other private beaches are open to the fee-paying general public and offer mattress or sun-lounger rental, showers and bar/restaurant facilities.

Safety. Côte d'Azur beaches are not especially dangerous, nor are they affected by great tidal variations. Always take care, however, to swim within the designated swimming areas. Where there are strong currents or the seabed falls away steeply, this is clearly indicated. Petty theft is probably a greater hazard, so never leave personal belongings unattended – especially on public beaches!

Topless bathing is totally accepted all along the Côte d'Azur, but nudism is only tolerated on certain beaches. A few have been designated for the sole use of naturists, principally around Saint-Tropez and the Ile du Levant – an island off the Var coast at Cavalaire. Further information is available from ADIL, cours le Roc, 87130 Châteauneuf-la-Forêt; tel. 55.57.01.61, or from any tourist office.

C

CAMPING (le camping)

Camping (for caravans and tents) is well catered for with a choice of two- to four-star sites. These vary in size from less than a 100 up to 5,000 pitches (*emplacements*) and most have showers, swimming pool, bike rental, tent rental and bar/restaurant. Some are adjacent to beaches and others attached to farms. Early booking in July/August is advisable. A free catalogue, *Camping and Caravaning*, is available from the Office départemental de tourisme, 1 esplanade John-Fitzgerald-Kennedy, 06000 Nice; tel. 93.92.82.82; or 8, avenue Colbert, 83000 Toulon; tel. 94.22.08.22.

Camping outside recognized sites (*camping sauvage*) is illegal and strictly prohibited. Watch out especially for signs saying *camping interdit* (camping forbidden).

Have you space for a tent/caravan?	**Avez-vous de la place pour une tente/caravane?**
May we camp on your land, please?	**Pouvons-nous camper sur votre terrain, s'il vous plaît?**

CAR RENTAL (location de voitures)
(See also DRIVING on p.124)

Car rental firms throughout the Côte d'Azur offer French and foreign makes. Local firms sometimes offer lower prices than the international companies, but may not let you return the car elsewhere, at convenient drop-off points.

To hire a car, you must have a driving licence (held for at least one year) and a passport. The minimum age varies from 20 to 23, depending on the firm, or more if an expensive model is involved. A substantial deposit (refundable) is usually required, unless you hold a credit card recognized by the car-rental company. You will also be asked for proof of your local or hotel address. Third party insurance is compulsory. For addresses, look in the telephone book under *Location de voitures*.

I'd like to rent a car today/tomorrow.	**Je voudrais louer une voiture aujourd'hui/demain.**
for one day/a week	**pour un jour/une semaine**

CLIMATE and CLOTHING

The Côte d'Azur enjoys a typical Mediterranean climate, that is to say hot dry summers, mild and wet in spring and autumn, and short winters that are usually quite mild but with cold spells. The area is also occasionally affected by the *mistral* – a strong cold wind that blows down the Rhône Valley and along the coast. Here are some average monthly temperatures:

		J	F	M	A	M	J	J	A	S	O	N	D
Air	°C	9	9	11	13	17	20	23	22	20	17	12	9
	°F	48	48	52	55	63	68	73	72	68	63	54	48
Sea	°C	13	13	13	15	17	21	24	25	23	20	17	14
	°F	55	55	55	59	63	70	75	77	73	68	63	57

Clothing. Dress is extremely casual, far more so than in other parts of France, and only the most formal of restaurants or casinos will require gentlemen to wear a jacket and tie (*tenue correcte*). Smart, casual attire is the norm. Jeans are universally acceptable.

Even in summer, a sweater or wrap is useful for cooler evenings, and a waterproof coat or jacket will be needed from October to April. Comfortable shoes (with a sturdy sole to cope with old cobbled streets) are advisable for sightseeing.

COMMUNICATIONS (See also OPENING HOURS on p.133 and TIME DIFFERENCES on p.136)

Post offices. They display a sign with a stylized bluebird and/or the words *Postes et Télécommunications*, P&T, or *La Poste*. In addition to normal mail service, you can make local or long-distance telephone calls, buy *télécartes* (phone-cards), and receive or send money at any post office. You can also buy stamps (*timbres*) and *télécartes* at tobacconists (*tabacs*, displaying a red cone outside).

Poste restante (general delivery). If you don't know ahead of time where you'll be staying, you can have your mail addressed to you in any town c/o *Poste restante*, *Poste centrale*. You can collect it for a small fee on presentation of your passport. Post can be sluggish in the summer months.

express (special delivery)	**par exprès**
airmail	**par avion**
registered	**en recommandé**
Have you any mail for ...?	**Avez-vous du courrier pour ...?**

Telephones. Many public telephones only accept *télécartes* (phone cards) which can be bought at post offices and tobacconists. Coin-operated phones will take 1F, 2F, 5F and 10F coins (have plenty of loose change ready – they gobble up the money!). You may make local or long distance calls from a public phone and also from cabins inside most post offices where the staff place the call for you.

For local and long-distance calls **within France** simply dial the eight-digit number, except when telephoning from the provinces to the Paris region when you should dial 16, wait for the tonality, then dial 1 followed by the eight-digit number; or when dialling the provinces from Paris when you should dial 16, wait for the tonality and dial the eight digit number.

For all **overseas** calls, dial 19, wait for the tonality, then dial the country code followed by the number. If the area code is prefixed by

0, omit the 0. Codes for the main English-speaking countries are as follows (others are listed in the front of telephone directories):

Australia:	19 61	**South Africa**:	19 27
Canada:	19 1	**UK**:	19 44
Irish Republic:	19 35	**US**:	19 1
New Zealand:	19 64		

To call the operator or directory enquiries, dial **12**. For international enquiries, dial **12 33** and the country code. A surcharge will normally be added for calls made from your hotel room.

COMPLAINTS (réclamation)

Complaints should be referred to the owner or manager of the establishment. If you fail to obtain a satisfactory reply, you can refer the matter to the nearest police station (*commissariat de police*). If the police cannot help, apply to the regional administration offices (*préfecture* or *sous-préfecture*), asking for the *service du tourisme*.

I'd like to make a complaint.　　　　**J'ai une réclamation à faire.**

CRIME (See also EMERGENCIES on p.127 and POLICE on p.134)

Inevitably, a prosperous area such as the Côte d'Azur attracts petty criminals and the major cities have some security problems, but incidents of violent crime against visitors are rare. Normal precautions apply. Try not to carry large amounts of cash, never leave valuables in your car and be on the look-out for pick-pockets, especially in crowds. Any loss or theft should be reported immediately to the nearest *commissariat de police* or *gendarmerie*.

CUSTOMS (douane) and ENTRY FORMALITIES

British visitors need only a passport to enter France, as do nationals of other EU countries and Switzerland. Others should check with the French embassy in their country for entry requirements.

As France is part of the European Union, free exchange of non-duty free goods for personal use is permitted between France, the **123**

UK and the Republic of Ireland. However, duty-free items are still subject to restrictions – check before you go.

For residents of non-EU countries, the restrictions into France and back into your own country are as follows: **France**: 400 cigarettes or 100 cigars or 500g tobacco, 1l spirits and 2l wine; **Australia**: 250 cigarettes or 250g of tobacco, 1l alcohol; **Canada**: 200 cigarettes and 50 cigars and 400g of tobacco, 1.1l spirits or wine or 8.5l beer; **New Zealand**: 200 cigarettes or 50 cigars or 250g tobacco, 4.5l wine or beer and 1.1l spirits; **South Africa**: 400 cigarettes and 50 cigars and 250g tobacco, 2l wine and 1l spirits; **USA**: 200 cigarettes and 100 cigars or 2kg tobacco, 1l wine or spirits.

D

DRIVING ON THE CÔTE D'AZUR
(See also CAR RENTAL on p.120)

To take a car into France you'll need: a valid driving licence, your car registration papers, insurance coverage (the green card is no longer obligatory for members of EU countries, but comprehensive cover is advisable), a red warning triangle and a set of spare bulbs.

Drivers and all passengers (back and front) are required by law to wear seat-belts (where fitted in the back). Children under the age of 10 may not travel in the front of the car. Driving on a foreign provisional licence is not permitted. The minimum driving age is 18.

Driving Regulations. Drive on the right, pass on the left. In built-up areas, give priority to vehicles coming from the right. The priority rule does not apply at roundabouts (*giratoires/rond-points*). Outside built-up areas, at such places as junctions marked by signs with a cross or yellow square on a white background, the more important of the two roads has the right of way.

Speed limits. When conditions are **dry**, the limit is 130kph (80mph) on toll motorways (expressways); 110kph (70mph) on dual-carriageways (divided highways); 90kph (55mph) on other country roads; and 45 or 60kph (30 or 35mph) in built-up areas.

Signposting is generally good. Tourist sights are usually highlighted with a brown symbol, making it very easy to distinguish them. A blue road sign directs you to an *autoroute* (motorway), a green one to a *route nationale* (RN: main road), and white to secondary 'D' roads. For ramblers, red and white markings at useful points indicate that the path being followed is on a 'GR' (*grandes randonnées*) trail.

Road conditions. Provence and the Côte d'Azur are well served with motorways, particularly if you are coming from Paris (the north/south axis), though roads can get clogged up in summer.

However, driving in France in general, and the Côte d'Azur in particular, is a pleasurable experience, except in the towns, at popular tourist sights, and areas heavily visited in summer. The roads are often less busy at lunchtime, when most people have stopped for a break, and also on Sunday when lorries are not allowed to travel.

Parking (*stationnement*). This is sometimes impossible in the height of summer, and often difficult the rest of the year. If possible, park outside the town centre and go by foot. Most major tourist sights have parking areas, but towns or villages often have worse problems.

You'll encounter two systems of parking – *zone bleue* (blue zone), and meters. If you want to leave your car in a *zone bleue*, you will need a *disque de stationnement*, a parking disc in the form of a cardboard clock which you can get from a petrol station, newsagent or stationer. Set it to show the time you arrived and it will indicate when you have to leave, then display it in the car. *Disque obligatoire* means 'disc obligatory'. Parking meters (*horodateurs*) are rife. *Stationnement interdit* means 'no parking'. Don't leave your car in a *zone piétonne* (pedestrian precinct), even less if the sign says *stationnement génant* (parking obstructive). A pictograph shows your car's fate ... being towed away.

Breakdowns (*panne*). There are emergency telephones approximately every 20km (12 miles) on main roads, connected directly to the local police stations which function round the clock. Elsewhere, dial 17, wherever you are, and the police can put you in touch with a garage that will come to your rescue – at a price, of course, so it's **125**

wise to take out international breakdown insurance before leaving home. Local garages usually provide towing facilities and spare parts for European cars. Always ask for an estimate before authorizing repairs, and expect to pay hefty value-added tax (*TVA*) on top.

Fuel and oil (*essence; huile*). Fuel is available as *super* (98-octane), *normale* (90-octane), *sans plomb* (lead free, 95-octane), *supergreen* (98-octane), and *gas-oil* (diesel). Most fuel stations are self-service. It's worth remembering to fill up on Saturday, since many garages close on Sunday. As petrol is quite expensive, it's best not to buy it on motorways; go to supermarkets instead (where it can be up to 15% cheaper).

accotements non stabilisés	soft shoulders
chaussée déformée	uneven road surface
déviation	diversion (detour)
péage	toll
priorité à droite	give way to traffic from right
ralentir	slow down
serrez à droite/à gauche	keep right/left
driving licence	**permis de conduire**
car registration papers	**carte grise**
Are we on the right road for ...?	**Sommes-nous sur la route de ...?**
Fill the tank, please.	**Le plein, s'il vous plaît.**
I've broken down.	**Ma voiture est en panne.**
There's been an accident.	**Il y a eu un accident.**

Fluid measures

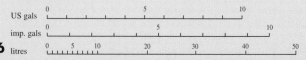

126 litres

ELECTRIC CURRENT
220-volt, 50-cycle AC is universal. British and American visitors should remember to buy an adaptor.

an adaptor plug   **une prise de raccordement**

EMBASSIES and CONSULATES
Most consulates are open from Monday to Friday, from 9 or 10am to 4 or 5pm with an hour or so off for lunch.

Australia: (embassy) 4, rue Jean-Rey, 75015 Paris; tel. (1) 40.59.33.00.

Canada: (embassy) 35, avenue Montaigne, 75008 Paris; tel. (1) 47.23.01.01.

UK: (consulate) 24, avenue du Prado, Marseille 13006; tel. 91.53.43.32.

Rep. of Ireland: (consulate) 152, boulevard John-Fitzgerald-Kennedy, Antibes; tel. 93.61.50.63.

USA: (consulate general) 12, boulevard Paul-Peytral, Marseille 13006; tel. 91.54.92.00.

(consulate): 36, rue du Maréchal Joffre, 06000 Nice; tel. 93.88.89.55.

EMERGENCIES (*urgence*) (See also Police on p.134)
In case of an emergency, dial **17** for the police (*police-secours*) and **18** for the fire brigade (*sapeurs-pompiers*), who also answer medical emergencies.

GUIDES and TOURS (*guide; excursion*)
With so much to see on the Côte d'Azur, some travellers enjoy joining a day or half-day coach trip taking in main attractions on the **127**

coast, the mountainous hinterland, or highlights of the Côte d'Azur nightlife. Enquire at your hotel or any *syndicat d'initiative* (tourist office, see p.136).

LANGUAGE

Southern French has a warm, charming accent, drawing out syllables in a way you don't hear elsewhere and placing more emphasis on the end of words or sentences. The usual nasal French 'en' ending becomes a hard 'ng' (*chien* sounds like *chieng*).

In addition, you'll hear all sorts of rolling, vaguely Italianate dialects, especially Niçois and Monégasque. You'll find a list of useful expressions listed on the inside front cover of this guide, and the Berlitz FRENCH PHRASE BOOK AND DICTIONARY covers almost all situations you're likely to encounter in your travels in France.

DAYS OF THE WEEK

Monday	**lundi**	Friday	**vendredi**
Tuesday	**mardi**	Saturday	**samedi**
Wednesday	**mercredi**	Sunday	**dimanche**
Thursday	**jeudi**		

MONTHS OF THE YEAR

January	**janvier**	July	**juillet**
February	**février**	August	**août**
March	**mars**	September	**septembre**
April	**avril**	October	**octobre**
May	**mai**	November	**novembre**
June	**juin**	December	**décembre**

NUMBERS

1	**un, une**	6	**six**
2	**deux**	7	**sept**
3	**trois**	8	**huit**
4	**quatre**	9	**neuf**

5	**cinq**	10	**dix**
11	**onze**	30	**trente**
12	**douze**	40	**quarante**
13	**treize**	50	**cinquante**
14	**quatorze**	60	**soixante**
15	**quinze**	70	**soixante-dix**
16	**seize**	71	**soixante et onze**
17	**dix-sept**	80	**quatre-vingt**
18	**dix-huit**	81	**quatre-vingt-un**
19	**dix-neuf**	90	**quatre-vingt-dix**
20	**vingt**	91	**quatre-vingt-onze**
21	**vingt et un**	100	**cent**
22	**vingt-deux**	1,000	**mille**

LAUNDRY and DRY CLEANING
(*blanchissage/ nettoyage à sec*)

There are plenty of fast-service dry cleaners (*blanchisserie* or *pressing*), but few launderettes (*laveries automatiques*) in France. Larger hotels have in-house laundry facilities – at a cost.

LOST PROPERTY (*objets trouvés*)

Check first at your hotel desk and if you have no success report the loss to the nearest *commissariat de police* or *gendarmerie* (see POLICE on p.134). If you have lost your passport, contact your consulate or embassy (see EMBASSIES AND CONSULATES on p.127).

I've lost my wallet/hand-bag/passport.

J'ai perdu mon porte-feuille/sac à main/passeport.

MEDIA

Newspapers and Magazines (*journal/revue*). *Nice Matin* and *Le Provençal* are the two leading local dailies, but newsagents in most coastal towns carry a selection of English-language papers (though **129**

these may arrive a day late and will be an international edition) and magazines. The Paris-based *International Herald Tribune* is also widely available.

Television and Radio. There are five main TV channels in France plus the cable channel Canal Plus. (In some areas it is also possible to receive some Italian, Swiss and German channels.) All programmes, except for a few late-night films, are in French and details are listed in local daily papers. In summer, some French radio stations transmit limited programmes in English, and Radio 104 transmits in English all day. BBC programmes can be received on short- or medium-wave radios.

MEDICAL CARE (See also EMERGENCIES on p.127)

Before you leave, make sure your health insurance policy covers illness or accident while on holiday. If not, ask your insurance representative, motoring association or travel agent about special holiday insurance plans. Visitors from EU countries with corresponding health insurance facilities are entitled to medical and hospital treatment under the French social security system. Before leaving home, ensure that you are eligible and have the appropriate forms. Doctors who belong to the French social security system (*médecins conventionnés*) charge the minimum.

If you're taken ill or have toothache, your hotel receptionist can probably recommend an English-speaking doctor or dentist; otherwise, ask at the *syndicat d'initiative*, or in an emergency, the *gendarmerie*. Chemists (*pharmacies*) display green crosses. Staff are helpful in dealing with minor ailments and can recommend a nurse (*infirmière*) if you need injections or other care.

In towns throughout the Côte d'Azur, there will be a chemist on duty at night on a rota system (*service de garde*). The name and address of the duty chemist is displayed in the window of other pharmacies – the *gendarmerie* or the local newspapers will also have it.

In Cannes, the Sunnybank Anglo-American Hospital is staffed by British nurses: **Sunnybank Hospital**, 133, avenue du Petit-Juas; tel. 93.68.29.96.

MONEY MATTERS

Currency (*monnaie*). For currency restrictions, see CUSTOMS AND ENTRY FORMALITIES on p.123. The *franc*, France's monetary unit (abbreviated F or FF) is divided into 100 *centimes*. Current coins include 5, 10, 20 and 50-centime pieces as well as 1, 2, 5, 10 and 20-franc pieces. Banknotes come in denominations of 20, 50, 100, 200 and 500 francs.

Many French people still like to express prices in 'old' francs (*anciens francs*) – although the system changed in the 1950s; 100 of them equal 1 'new' franc. In shops, however, only new francs are referred to.

Banks and Currency-Exchange Offices (*banque; bureau de change*). Hours may vary, but most banks are open Monday to Friday from 9 to 11.30am and 1.30 to 5pm. Some currency-exchange offices operate on Saturday as well. At Monte Carlo, a *bureau de change* opposite the Casino is open every day.

Your hotel will usually change currency or traveller's cheques into francs, but the rate is not favourable – nor is it in shops and casinos where traveller's cheques are often accepted. Always take your passport along when you go to change money.

Credit Cards (*carte de credit*). Most hotels, smarter restaurants, some boutiques, car-rental firms and tourist-related businesses in towns accept the major credit cards.

Traveller's cheques (*chèque de voyage*). Hotels, travel agents and many shops accept them, although the exchange rate is invariably better at a bank. Don't forget to take your passport when going to cash a traveller's cheque. Eurocheques are also widely accepted.

Prices (*prix*). The cost of living on the Côte d'Azur is generally high, but it is possible to have a good time on a budget if you choose carefully. (The further you get away from the coast, the more likely you are to find reasonably priced hotels and restaurants.)

Official prices are always posted prominently in public establishments, including cafés, bars, hotels and restaurants.

Could you give me some (small) change?	**Pouvez-vous me donner de la (petite) monnaie?**
I want to change some pounds/dollars.	**Je voudrais changer des livres sterling/des dollars.**
Do you accept traveller's cheques?	**Acceptez-vous les chèques de voyage?**
Can I pay with this credit card?	**Puis-je payer avec cette carte de crédit?**

PLANNING YOUR BUDGET

The following are some prices in French francs (F). However, they must be regarded as approximate; inflation in France, as elsewhere, continues to rise steadily.

Babysitters. 35-65F per hour, 200-350F per day.

Bicycle and moped rental. Bicycle 120F per day, moped 150F, minimum deposit; 1,000F bicycle; 5,000F moped.

Boat rental. Motor boat 600-900F for four persons per day, sailing boat (medium) 2,000F for four persons per weekend.

Camping. 120-220F per night for four persons with tent or caravan (trailer).

Car rental. Group A (e.g. Renault Clio) 545F per day, 1,925F per week. Group B (e.g. Renault 19) 685F per day, 2,500F per week. Group C (e.g. Renault 25) 830F per day, 3,285F per week. All rates include unlimited mileage. Add 33.33% tax.

Cigarettes. French 10F per packet of 20, foreign 14F, cigars 3-70F each.

Entertainment. Cinema 40F, admission to discotheque 80-100F, Casino admission 60-70F, cabaret 100F upwards (including meal).

Guides. 500F for half day, 900F per day, 125-150F for each additional hour.

Hotels (per double room). **** 700-1,000F, *** 350-800F, ** 250-400F, * 150-250F. Youth hostel 65-75F.

Meals and drinks. Continental breakfast 30-60F, tourist menu 70-120F, lunch/dinner in fairly good establishment 150-200F, coffee 6F, whisky or cocktail 25-35F, beer/soft drink 15F, cognac 25F, bottle of wine 55F and up.

Museums. 10-40F. (See also MUSEUM AND ART GALLERY HIGHLIGHTS on p.60 for more details.)

Sports. Windsurf board about 60F an hour, 600F a week, instruction (with board, one lesson per day during one week) 400-500F, waterskiing (6 minutes) 100F, tennis 50F an hour for a court, golf 120F (9-hole), 250F (18-hole) per day.

OPENING HOURS (heures d'ouverture)

Opening hours vary greatly, but the main feature is the long Mediterranean lunch break when most shops close on the dot at noon and do not open again much before 4pm.

Banks are usually open Monday to Friday from 9am to noon and 2 to 5pm. Some may close on Monday or open on Saturday morning. Banking facilities are available at Nice and Marseille airport (see AIRPORTS on p.119) from early morning to late at night (depending on flight arrivals and departures).

Main post offices are open Monday to Friday and Saturday morning 9am to noon and 2 to 5pm . In large towns they may open earlier and close later.

Groceries, **bakeries** and **food shops** are open approximately Monday to Saturday 8am to noon and 2, 3 or 4pm to 7 or 8pm. Many open Sunday morning and close one day during the week, often Monday.

Museums and art galleries are open from 10am to noon and 2 to 6pm (sometimes later in summer). Many state-owned museums close on Tuesday. Check before visiting. (See also MUSEUM AND ART GALLERY HIGHLIGHTS on p.60 for further details.)

PHOTOGRAPHY (*la photographie*) and VIDEO
(*le caméscope*)

The coast is a photographer's dream, with plenty of light, varied scenery and colours of every intensity from soft pastel shades to the most vibrant hues. Certain museums will give you permission to photograph inside.

All popular film makes and sizes are available in France. Rapid development is possible, but quite expensive.

Camcorders are increasingly popular in France, where you'll find most types of tape. However, it's a good idea to stock up on film before setting off.

I'd like a film for this camera/video camera.	**J'aimerais un film pour cet appareil/ce caméscope.**
a black-and-white film	**un film noir et blanc**
a film for colour prints	**un film couleurs**
a colour-slide film	**un film de diapositives**
How long will it take to develop this film?	**Combien de temps faut-il pour développer ce film?**

POLICE (*la police*)

In cities and larger towns you'll see the blue-uniformed **police municipale**; they are the local police force who keep order, investigate crime and direct traffic. Outside of the main towns are the **gendarmes** – they wear blue trousers and black jackets with white belts and are also responsible for traffic and crime investigation.

The **CRS** police (*Compagnies Républicaines de Sécurité*) are a national security force responsible to the Ministry of the Interior, and are called in for emergencies and special occasions.

Call **17** anywhere in France for police assistance.

Where's the nearest police station?	**Où est le poste de police le plus proche?**

PUBLIC HOLIDAYS (*jour férié*)

1 January	**Jour de l'An**	New Year's Day
1 May	**Fête du Travail**	Labour Day
8 May	**Fête de la Libération**	Victory Day (1945)
14 July	**Fête Nationale**	Bastille Day
15 August	**Assomption**	Assumption
1 November	**Toussaint**	All Saints' Day
11 November	**Anniversaire de l'Armistice**	Armistice Day
25 December	**Noël**	Christmas
Movable Dates:	**Lundi de Pâques**	Easter Monday
	Ascencion	Ascension
	Lundi de Pentecôte	Whit Monday

R

RELIGION

France is a predominantly Roman Catholic country. Ask your hotel receptionist or the local tourist office for information about the location and times of services in English. There are English-speaking Protestant churches and synagogues in Cannes, Menton, Monaco, Nice and Saint-Raphaël. Non-Catholic services are called *cultes*.

Where is the Protestant church/synagogue?	**Où se trouve le temple protestant/la synagogue?**

S

SMOKING

Smoking is now prohibited in all state-owned buildings such as post offices and government buildings, and public places such as theatres, cinemas and museums. Restaurants are required to set aside an area for non-smokers and smoking is not allowed on buses.

TIME DIFFERENCES

France follows Greenwich Mean Time + 1, and in spring the clocks are put forward one hour. If your country does the same, the time difference remains constant for most of the year.

L.A.	Chicago	New York	London	**Nice**	Sydney
3am	5am	6am	11am	**noon**	8pm

TIPPING

A 10 to 15% service charge is generally included automatically in hotel and restaurant bills. Rounding off the overall bill helps round off friendships with waiters, too. It is also in order to hand the bell-boys, doormen, filling station attendants, etc, a coin or two for their services. The list below gives some suggestions as to what to leave.

Hotel porter, per bag	5F
Hotel maid, per week	20-50F
Lavatory attendant	1-2F
Waiter	5-10% (optional)
Taxi driver	10-15% (optional)
Tour guide, half day	10-20F

TOURIST INFORMATION OFFICES
(office du tourisme; syndicat d'initiative)

French national tourist offices can help you plan your holiday and will supply you with a wide range of colourful, informative maps and brochures. Some addresses:

Canada: 1981 McGill College Avenue, Suite 490, Esso Tower, Montreal, Quebec. H3A 2W9; tel. (514) 288 4264.

1 Dundas Street West, Suite 2405, PO Box 8, Toronto, Ontario. M5G 1Z3; tel. (416) 593 4717.

UK: 178 Piccadilly, London W1V 0AL; tel. (071) 493 6594.

USA: 645 North Michigan Avenue, Suite 430, Chicago, Illinois 60611; tel. (312) 337 6301.

9401 Wilshire Boulevard, Room 840, Beverly Hills, California 90212; tel. (213) 272 2661.

610 5th Avenue, New York, NY 10020; tel. (212) 757 1125.

1 Hallidie Plaza, San Francisco, California 94102; tel. (415) 986 4174.

Local tourist information offices (*syndicat d'initiative*) are invaluable sources of information in all French towns. They are found near the town's centre and often have a branch at the railway station. Opening hours vary, but the general rule is 8.30 or 9am to noon and from 2 to 6 or 7pm, every day except Sunday. A few addresses:

Cannes: Office du tourisme, Palais des festivals, La Croisette; tel. 93.39.24.53.

Marseilles: Office municipal du tourisme, 4, La Canebière; tel. 91.54.91.11.

Monaco: Direction du tourisme et des congrès, 2a, boulevard des Moulins; tel. 92.16.61.16.

Nice: Office du tourisme, 1, esplanade John-Fitzgerald-Kennedy and at the airport (parking Ferber). Syndicat d'initiative, central railway station; tel. 93.87.07.07.

TRANSPORT

Buses (*autobus*, *autocar*). There are excellent urban and inter-town services all along the Côte d'Azur. Pay as you enter or buy a book of tickets from the driver. Inspectors board buses regularly to check tickets. Further information can be obtained from the bus station (*gare routière*) in all major towns.

Taxis are widely available but not all have meters. If in doubt, ask the cost of the trip before getting in.

Trains. The SNCF network along the coast is fast and efficient. Ask about various categories of tickets for tourists, children, families, under 26s and OAPs. Eurail passes and Inter-rail cards are valid.

In **Nice**, the 'little white train' is in service throughout the year except from 1 January to the start of Carnival Week in February, and runs every 20 minutes from 10am to 7pm daily except Monday, when it starts at 2pm. (Duration: 40 minutes; cost: 20F)

Boat ferries operate from *gares maritimes* (ferry stations) at Cannes for the Iles de Lérins; and for the Iles d'Hyères – Toulon, Hyères (Port d'Hyères or La Tour Fondue at Giens), Port de Miramar, Le Lavandou and Cavalaire. In addition you can take a *bateau-taxi* from Hyères (tel. 94.58.31.19).

TRAVELLERS WITH DISABILITIES

So far, the Côte d'Azur has done little to help the disabled traveller, although things are changing, and more and more airports, hotels, museums and other establishments are better equipped to assist your needs. A tour operator will be able to help you tailor your holiday, and regional tourist offices will also be able to provide valuable information (see TOURIST INFORMATION OFFICES on p.136).

TRAVELLING TO THE CÔTE D'AZUR

By car. The 1,200km (750 miles) direct autoroute trip from Calais to Nice (via Reims and bypassing Paris) can take as little as 15 hours, or you can stay overnight at one of the autoroute hotels. However, *péage* (toll) fees are expensive and drivers who prefer a cheaper, more leisurely drive often opt to use both autoroutes and main roads.

By coach. From London Victoria Station: twice a week in season to Nice and Cannes, and once a week year-round to Marseilles. Journey time roughly 23 hours.

By train. From Paris the TGV (high-speed train) takes 5 hours to Marseille and 7 hours to Nice, but there is a supplementary charge. For more economical fares, French railways (SNCF) offer attractive discounts and period tickets for unlimited travel; and special concessionary tickets for overseas visitors under 26 travelling to the Côte d'Azur. Eurail and Inter-rail are valid on all routes, but a supplement may have to be paid on some trains.

By Motor-rail. SNCF operates a direct overnight service from Dover to Marseille and Nice, via Paris. Passengers without a car may also use this service.

WEIGHTS and MEASURES

France uses the metric system. The charts below should help you convert from metric to Imperial. (For fluid measures see p.126.)

Weight

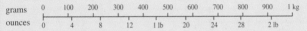

Length

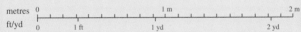

Distance

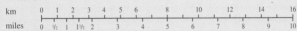

Temperature

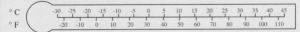

YOUTH HOSTELS (*auberge de jeunesse*)

Your national youth hostel association can give you all the details, or contact the Fédération Unie des Auberges de Jeunesse, 10, rue Notre-Dame-de-Lorette, 75009 Paris; tel. (1) 42.85.55.40.

Index

Where there is more than one set of references, the one in **bold** refers to the main entry. Page numbers in *italic* refer to an illustration.

143

Berlitz – pack the world in your pocket!

Africa
Algeria
Kenya
Morocco
South Africa
Tunisia

Asia, Middle East
China
Egypt
Hong Kong
India
Indonesia
Japan
Jerusalem
Malaysia
Singapore
Sri Lanka
Taiwan
Thailand

Australasia
Australia
New Zealand
Sydney

Austria, Switzerland
Austrian Tyrol
Switzerland
Vienna

Belgium, The Netherlands
Amsterdam
Brussels

British Isles
Channel Islands
Dublin
Ireland
London
Scotland

Caribbean, Latin America
Bahamas
Bermuda
Cancún and Cozumel
Caribbean
French West Indies
Jamaica
Mexico
Mexico City/Acapulco
Puerto Rico
Rio de Janeiro
Southern Caribbean
Virgin Islands

Central and Eastern Europe
Budapest
Hungary
Moscow and St Petersburg
Prague

France
Brittany
Châteaux of the Loire
Côte d'Azur
Dordogne
Euro Disney Resort
France
Normandy
Paris
Provence

Germany
Berlin
Munich
Rhine Valley

Greece, Cyprus and Turkey
Athens
Corfu
Crete
Cyprus
Greek Islands
Istanbul
Rhodes
Turkey

Italy and Malta
Florence
Italy
Malta
Milan and the Lakes
Naples
Rome
Sicily
Venice

North America
Alaska Cruise Guide
Boston
California
Canada
Disneyland and the Theme Parks of Southern California
Florida
Greater Miami
Hawaii
Los Angeles
Montreal
New Orleans
New York
San Francisco
Toronto
USA
Walt Disney World and Orlando
Washington

Portugal
Algarve
Lisbon
Madeira

Scandinavia
Copenhagen
Helsinki
Oslo and Bergen
Stockholm
Sweden

Spain
Barcelona
Canary Islands
Costa Blanca
Costa Brava
Costa del Sol
Costa Dorada and Tarragona
Ibiza and Formentera
Madrid
Mallorca and Menorca
Seville

IN PREPARATION
Bali and Lombok
Bruges and Ghent
Cuba
Edinburgh
Israel
Portugal
Spain

019/506 RV